MENTAL HEALTH ON THE COMMUNITY COLLEGE CAMPUS

Second Edition

Edited by

Gerald Amada

UNIVERSITY
PRESS OF
AMERICA

LANHAM • NEW YORK • LONDON

Copyright © 1985 by

University Press of America,® Inc.

4720 Boston Way
Lanham, MD 20706

3 Henrietta Street
London WC2E 8LU England

Library of Congress Cataloging in Publication Data
Main entry under title:

Mental health on the community college campus.

Includes bibliographies.
1. Minority college students—Mental health
services—California—San Francisco.   2. Minority
students—Mental health services—California—San
Francisco.   3. Community college students—Mental
health services—California—San Francisco.   4. City
College of San Francisco—Students—Mental health
services. I. Amada, Gerald. [DNLM: 1. Mental Health
Services. 2. Student Health Services. WA 353 M549]
RC451.4.S7M44   1985   378'.19712   85-17920
ISBN 0-8191-4914-4 (alk. paper)
ISBN 0-8191-4915-2 (pbk. : alk. paper)

All University Press of America books are produced on acid-free
paper which exceeds the minimum standards set by the National
Historical Publications and Records Commission.

To Marcia, Robin, Naomi, Laurie, and Eric,

with love and appreciation

iii

iv

CONTENTS

CONTENTS (Cont'd.)

Page

FOREWORD

In this collection of articles Gerald Amada and his colleagues at City College of San Francisco have set forth their methods of reaching students and responding to their mental health and family needs. Mental health programs are exceedingly rare in community colleges, but the experience at City College confirms both the cost effectiveness and life effectiveness values of mental health efforts on behalf of students.

The authors recount the struggles of program growth and development. They spell out the kind of commitment required to establish and maintain a new service in times of competition for diminishing resources. The work is especially significant because of the diverse and racially mixed student body at City College, and the articles address the special sensitivities required for understanding and serving minority students. The accounts also provide insight into the needs of older students and those who carry responsibility for family support.

The Zellerbach Family Fund, a private foundation, supported this clinical and outreach program because the Board believed that such mental health services could provide essential help to a population of students at high risk, and that students are entitled to a comprehensive and integrated health service that includes psychotherapeutic components. The Board further believed that having mental health services easily available could reduce school dropout and provide guidance that would prevent academic failure and the family breakups that frequently follow school-induced stress and failure.

It was recognized that foundations can and should provide risk capital and additional funds at crucial times when public monies are restricted. The existence of a stable Mental Health Service at City College is testimony to the values of partnership efforts involving the resources of private foundations and public bodies.

It is to the credit of the administrative leadership at City College that they gave their moral and financial support to this program. There was some continuing risk that the program design might not meet students needs. Further, City College had to rank the priority of this servcie with respect to other programs that also served students. Fortunately, the students determined the value of the service by their involvement and their support.

vii

There are many colleagues among the staff and faculty of City College who are entitled to my appreciation for their help and cooperation. I wish to thank them as a collectivity and also to make mention of two instructors in particular, Glen Nance and Tom Velasquez, who served as spokespersons for the Mental Health Program at crucial points in its historical development.

I naturally wish to thank former President Kenneth Washington, President Carlos Ramirez and the Board of Governors of City College for their confidence in the Mental Health Program. In many respects, the success of the program is a tribute to their enlightened and progressive leadership.

The Mental Health Program relies heavily upon a dedicated classified staff for direction and assistance. Amelia Lippi and Jim Cunningham have been important cogs in the wheel that makes the program run effectively.

I wish to express my appreciation to the students of City College, who never cease to challenge and stimulate me.

This book is for Marcia, Robin, Naomi, Laurie and Eric: with love.

Gerald Amada, Editor
San Francisco, CA 1985

CONTRIBUTORS

Gerald Amada, Ph.D.,   - Co-Director of the Mental Health Program,
                          City College of San Francisco

Judith Carey, M.P.H.   - Former Head, Student Health Services, City
                          College of San Francisco

Andrew Curry, M.S.W.   - Former consultant to the Mental Health
                          Program, City College of San Francisco

Kenneth Davis, M.S.W.   - Former stff psychotherapist, Mental Health
                          Program, City College of San Francisco

Sam Edwards, Jr., M.S.W. - Staff psychotherapist, Mental Health
                          Program, City College of San Francisco

Art Hom, M.S.W.   - Former staff psychotherapist, Mental
                          Health Program, City College of San
                          Francisco

Alan Leavitt, M.A.   - Former Director of the Mental Health
                          Program, City College of San Francisco

Andrea Polk, Ph.D.   - Staff psychotherapist with the Mental
                          Health Program, City College of San
                          Francisco

Annette R. Pont-Gwire, Ph.D. - Staff psychotherapist with the
                          Mental Health Program, City College of
                          San Francisco

E. Lance Rogers, Ed.D. - Former Chairperson of the Physics
                          Department , City College of San Francisco

Jacqueline Swartz   - Former staff writer, City College of San
                          Francisco

ix

ACKNOWLEDGMENTS

This book is a by-product of a community college mental health program which was organized and sustained through the generous assistance of a great many people and organizations.

The Zellerbach Family Fund of San Francisco and its Executive Director, Ed Nathan, provided the original grant which established the City College of San Francisco Mental Health Program in 1970. I wish to acknowledge my deep gratitude to this foundation for the constant support and venturesome spirit it provided in making the success of the program possible.

I am indebted to the Westside Community Mental Health Services of San Francisco which provided supplemental funding and administrative sponsorship to the Mental Health Program in its earliest years. I would like to extend special thanks to the administrators of that agency who provided timely and vital leadership to the Mental Health Program: Dr. William Pierce, Dr. Ira Plotinsky and Dr. William Goldman.

I want to express my gratitude to the Bothin Helping Fund of San Francisco for its windfall and generous grant at a time when the Mental Health Program was faced with the prospect of serious cutbacks in personnel and services. Genevieve di San Faustino, Vice President of this foundation, deserves special appreciation for the decisive and exuberant assistance she extended to the program.

Progress Foundation, Inc. of San Francisco performed many rescue operations for the Mental Health Program, particularly by providing the program, over a period of several years, its administrative aegis. Heartfelt thanks are due to the administrators of this agency who gave unstintingly of their time and effort in behalf of the program: Dr. Patricia Caughey, Steve Harover and Steve Fields.

I am extremely grateful to Dr. Carl Zlatchin of Mt. Zion Hospital, San Francisco, whose intercession in behalf of the Mental Health Program was pivotal to its eventual adoption as a permanent college service. I owe a debt of gratitude to another "Mt. Zion" psychologist, Dr. Donald Cliggett, who in the past supervised my clinical work with great patience and sensitivity.

In most respects, the Mental Health Program is the brainchild of one of its original organizers, Alan Leavitt. To Alan I wish to extend my respect and appreciation.

There are many colleagues among the staff and faculty of City College who are entitled to my appreciation for their help and cooperation. I wish to thank them as a collectivity and also to make mention of two instructors in particular, Glen Nance and Tom Velasquez, who served as spokespersons for the Mental Health Program at crucial points in its historical development.

I naturally wish to thank former President Kenneth Washington, President Carlos Ramirez and the Board of Governors of City College for their confidence in the Mental Health Program. In many respects, the success of the program is a tribute to their enlightened and progressive leadership.

The Mental Health Program relies heavily upon a dedicated classified staff for direction and assistance. Amelia Lippi and Jim Cunningham have been important cogs in the wheel that makes the program run effectively.

I wish to express my appreciation to the students of City College, who never cease to challenge and stimulate me.

This book is for Marcia, Robin, Naomi, Laurie and Eric: with love.

Gerald Amada, Editor
San Francisco, CA 1985

I

ORGANIZING A COMMUNITY COLLEGE

MENTAL HEALTH PROGRAM

Gerald Amada

This chapter will attempt to describe and explain the complex process of establishing and maintaining a mental health program on an urban community college campus -- City College of San Francisco. The unique background of this program was profoundly affected by the particular college and city in which it is located.

City College of San Francisco

City College of San Francisco is a two-year community college of approximately 14,000 day students and 9,000 evening students. It has an open admissions policy. It offers two basic programs: (1) an academic curriculum designed to enable students to transfer to a four-year college or university, and (2) vocational or semiprofessional training programs, including police science, dental assistance, and hotel/restaurant management. Particular emphasis in recent years has been placed upon the recruitment and tutoring ofr disadvantaged people who would otherwise not attend college.

City College, like other urban colleges, has a student population which reflects the diversity of the city itself. Statistics for the Spring 1985 semester indicate that more than one-half of the students were from ethnic minorities. 31% were White, 40% Asian, 11% Black, 9% Latin American, 7% Filipino and 2% other origins. In 1970 (the year of the inception of the Mental Health Program) 17 per cent of all students had family incomes under $300 per month; another 15 per cent had total family incomes ranging from $301 to $500 per month.

1

In the Spring 1985 semester the median ages of all students, day and evening, was 27 years. As Carey and Rogers point out (1973), this youthful, urban student population is a group which is particularly susceptible to a variety of medical and social problems, including venereal disease, drug and alcohol abuse, and unwanted pregnancy. Many City College students have grown up handicapped by linguistic and cultural backgrounds that are sharply different from the White, middle-class world they are entering, perhaps for the first time, as college students. These differences are compounded by financial and personal problems, poor housing, criminal records, heavy drug use, an impulsive live-for-the moment orientation developed in reaction to the largely ungratifying world in which they have always lived. For many students, schools are hostile and frustrating places.

For the younger student, City College represents a transition from high school to the assumption of an adult role in the community. In addition to mounting responsibilities, the student will have to cope with the complexities of sexual liberation and the prevalent use of drugs -- issues around which he must develop a personal philosophy and courage. The older student may face a different set of dilemmas: academic skills may be rusty, although a wealth of personal experiences can be a great asset. Yet all students will face a formidable world, often with much uncertainty and fear.

The City of San Francisco

City College is strongly shaped and influenced by the city in which it resides. San Francisco, like so many other large American cities, is constantly undergoing many processes of social change. The city´s 1975 population of 776,000 was crowded into 45.4 square miles: the highest population density in the state and one of the highest in the nation (14,707 per square mile).

San Francisco is unique in its multi-racial and ethnic mix, with more "other nonwhite" than Black population. Ethnic group estimates for 1975 follow the trends experienced during the decade 1960 to 1970, with a decrease, 61,186 or 12.0% in the White population and an increase of 13,212 or 6.5% in the nonwhite groups in 1975 over 1970. Blacks gained nearly one and one-half per cent, while the Chinese showed a numerical increase of 4,504, Filipinos 4,406 and other nonwhite groups, 1985.

Although San Francisco has a declining population (47,974 or 6.7% from 1970 to 1975), it suffers from chronic housing and job shortages. The housing problems are compounded by property costs which have risen rapidly in the last decade. It is estimated that nearly 16 per cent of San Francisco households pay between 25 and 34 per cent of their income for rent and about 30 per cent pay more than 35 per cent of their income for rent.

In addition to changes in the ethnic composition of the city, there have been other changes in the city's population structure. San Francisco's residents are becoming, synchronously, younger and older. San Francisco consistently has a higher death rate than California and surrounding counties chiefly because of the age structure of its population. In 1975, almost 15% of its population was at least 65 years of age.

Also reflecting the age and ethnic composition of the city are the leading causes of death for its residents. While the four leading causes of death (diseases of the heart, malignant neoplasms, cerebrovascular disease and accidents) are the same as those statewide and nationally, it is significant that the fifth leading cause of death in the city is cirrhosis of the liver. This compares with a seventh rank nationally and a sixth rank in California for this disease. Suicide is the seventh leading cause of death in San Francisco as compared to its tenth rank nationally.

In 1975, San Francisco had one of the highest case rates of tuberculosis in the country. Statistics of the Department of Public Health reveal an overall case rate of 51.7 per 100,000 (345 cases), with the Filipino (226.8 per 100,000) and Chinese (101.3 per 100,000) ethnic groups showing the highest rates of this disease.

In the late 1960's, SanFrancisco was a leading center of counter-culture activity. Thousands of young people descended upon the city in hopes of a better life than was offered in the suburbs of America. Unfortunately, many personal tragedies resulted from the huge influx of teenage youth. Harassment from the law enforcement agencies left many with criminal records. Others suffered from severe drug abuse and the terror instilled by the oppressively open sexual mores which prevailed in the groups with which they associated. Many are still struggling to re-enter the mainstream of the economic and social systems. Some of that once rebellious group became students of City College.

Rationales for College Mental Health Services

Farnsworth (1966), using a variety of data at Harvard University (a relatively low-risk student population), estimated that for every 10,000 students:
1,000 will have emotional conflicts of sufficient severity to warrant professional help.

3

300 to 400 will have feelings of depression severe enough to impair their efficiency.

100 to 200 will be apathetic and unable to organize their efforts - "I can't make myself want to work."

20 to 50 will be so adversely affected by past family experiences that they will be unable to control their impulses.

15 to 25 will become ill enough to require treatment in a mental hospital.

5 to 20 will attempt suicide, of whom one or more will succeed.

Recognition of the debilitating emotional stress of many students and the need for colleges and universities to take affirmative measures to cope effectively with that stress was expressed by President William A. Stearns of Amherst over 100 years ago.

The breaking down of the health of students, especially in the spring of the year, which is exceedingly common, involving the necessity of leaving college in many instances, and crippling the energies and destroying the prospects of not a few who remain is in my opinion wholly unnecessary if proper measures could be taken to prevent it.
(Stearns, 1869, in Farnsworth, 1957)

Although the rationales commonly adduced in the advocacy of college mental health services tend to dramatize the psychopathology and morbidity of students, such one-sided championing is rather outmoded and potentially insulting to students. As indicated by Binger (1961), the fact that about 10 per cent of students may require professional assistance during their college careers, does not mean that:

those who seek help are necessarily sicker than those who do not. They may simply recognize and acknowledge difficulties which others try to deny.

Certainly a campus mental health service must be amply prepared to respond to students who suffer from severe psychological stresses and vicissitudes. It must be a dependable and useful refuge for those students who have chronic personality disorders, including those of the psychotic variety. On the other hand, a mental health service should not be instituted on the basis of a spurious and self-defeating notion that it is a facility which will be beneficial solely or even primarily to

4

to "sick" students. To identify the utility of a psychological service in such a tendentious manner might seriously discourage the utilization of such a program even by those students who truly suffer from serious psychiatric disorders and would certainly dissuade the more well functioning students who periodically require help with transient psychological difficulties from seeking assitance.

The experience of higher education has been recognized by Freedman as one which has the potential for animating an:

appreciation of the complexity of people and social events, openness to new experiences, flexiblity in thinking, compassion in judgment of people, and the like. These changes are large in some students, small in others. But few go through college without acquiring at least a tinge of this liberalization and the social consequences of such changes are enormous.
(Freedman, 1967)

Jade Snow Wong, an alumna of City College of San Francisco, in her poignant autobiographical book, Fifth Chinese Daughter, states in personal terms how two years of college critically reorganized her personality.

Hand in hand with a growing awareness of herself and her personal world (Wong writes of herself in the third person), there was developing in her an awareness of and a feeling for the larger world beyond the familiar pattern. The two years had made her a little wiser in the ways of the world, a little more realistic, less of a dreamer, and she hoped more of a personality.
(Wong, 1945)

If the experience of learning in college is dynamic and serves as a catalyst to further personal growth and understanding for many students, a college mental health program can legitimately be predicated upon the rightful aspirations of such students to further experiment and self-discover, in a credible psychological milieu within the educational institution itself.

The City College Mental Health Program

The Mental Health Program had its obscure genesis in the Student Health Service of City College. In 1968, the Student Health Service was staffed by only one health practitioner, a public health nurse (PHN). Although her official responsibilities were to provide medical-nursing services exclusively, the PHN was continually besieged by students who

5

were plagued with a wide variety of complex psychological difficulties. Her plaint, at the time, was that the only available means of assisting students was by means of referring them to community psychiatric clinics, a procedure which was frequently undesirable and abortive. In her own words, referring students in psychological crises to off-campus agencies too often meant:

> time-consuming searches for proper assistance, long waiting lists, endless red-tape and financial hassles. In addition, many students have found the process of applying for services elsewhere an awesomely formidable challenge, due to feelings of self-stigma, which they would prefer to avoid. Usually, by the time adequate assistance has materialized, it has been too late, and the student's whole semester is at stake; one factor which accounts for the unusually high rates of leaves of absence each semester.

Based upon the PHN's own findings, which were solidly substantiated by available epidemiological research of college students on other campuses, a pilot project was conducted in the Spring of 1969. The objectives of the pilot project were: (1) to centralize psychological services on campus, and (2) to determine the extent of potential utilization of such a program. To implement this study, a third-year psychiatric resident with the San Francisco Mental Health Services was assigned to the Student Health Service for the Spring Semester. His responsibilities included: (a) direct psychological services to the PHN, faculty and administration, in dealing with the emotional problems of students, and (c) psychiatric liaison services to community agencies to facilitiate mutual referrals of students for psychotherapy.

The Student Health Service maintained an open intake policy, seeing all students who applied and seeing them soon after application. The psychiatric resident spent the majority of his time in direct psychotherapeutic work with students. He also spent a generous amount of time in consultation with college personnel. Deliberately, minimal time was allotted to activities such as processing applications, history-taking, psychological assessment and record-keeping.

At the end of the Spring semester, 98 different students had been served by the program. This group received a total of 253 sessions. Although these 98 students comprised only a miniscule proportion of the total number of 14,000 day students enrolled in 1969, these figures are impressive for several reasons: (1) the program was new and, therefore, the student body initially had little knowledge of its availability or whereabouts, (2) the psychiatric resident, who was the sole provider of psychological services, was new to the campus himself and had had little time to familiarize himself with those programs and personnel which could serve as effective sources of student referrals to the Student Health Service (as was pointed out in subsequent years, vast numbers of college personnel knew virtually nothing of the pilot study which was conducted in 1969), and (3) as Farnsworth (1964) suggests, the extent to which students utilize the Student Health Service will depend in part on the manner in which they perceive the service and its usefulness to them. Since one semester was clearly a too abbreviated period of time in which to engender student trust in the usefulness of the program, the intake figures for the Spring semester of 1969 were not regarded as a valid index of future utilization of the psychological services.

Based upon the relative success of the demonstration project, the PHN next proceeded to contact major community hospitals and psychiatric clinics, hoping to enlist their support in organizing and staffing a formal mental health clinic on campus. The earliest responses from personnel of these organizations were friendly to the concept of an on-campus psychological service at City College but quite unreceptive to bearing certain practical sacrifices in order to bring such a program to fruition. At best, those agencies intimated that they could provide consultation services to college personnel, if such a bilateral arrangement were practicable.

In 1969, the PHN submitted grant requests to local foundations for funding of a "demonstration" Mental Health Program at City College. The Zellerbach Family Fund of San Francisco awarded a grant which was supplemented by funding from the National Institute of Mental Health. This supplemental grant was provided under the auspices of the Westside Mental Health Services (a local consortium of mental health agencies) which assumed, with a community psychiatric clinic, co-sponsorship of the Mental Health Program. The Mental Health Program began serving students in January, 1970.

With the advent of the Mental Health Program, several service priorities were established:

1. To deal effectively and rapidly with basically well functioinig students in psychological crisis.

2. To refer those students in need of services that were not available at the college to other community resources.

7

3. To provide supportive services on an ongoing basis to some severely disturbed students needing such assistance.

4. To help students learn as much as possible about the maintenance of mental health and the minimization of emotional stress.

5. To make consultation services readily available to all college personnel, with respect to their concerns about the mental health needs of students.

In order to implement these service goals, the following guidelines and policies were adopted: there would be no charge for services and intake was to be entirely voluntary; i.e., no student would be seen against his or her wishes. All information was to be held in strict confidence within the Student Health Service, kept separate from all other student records. The importance of the preservation of confidentiality applied also to the question of whether or not a particular student had come to the clinic at all. The program would maintain an "open" intake seeing any regularly enrolled student who applied as soon as possible after application. Waiting periods and waiting lists would be kept to a minimum.

The general goal of psychological services was to promote personal growth by giving students an opportunity to explore problems which interfered with studies, work, and relationships with family and friends. Those clinical staff recruited to the program were specially sought for their proven skills, sensitivity and experience in handling acute problems. The ethnic composition of the staff would approximate the composition of the multiethnic student body (Carey, Swartz and Leavitt, 1971). This practice would hopefully encourage minority students to utilize the psychological services in numbers proportionate to their percentages in the student body as a whole.

The mainstay of the program was to be short-term crisis-oriented services to insure the availability of immediate appointments for a maximum number of students. Although it was expected that most students would receive individual psychotherapeutic services, provisions were made for group therapy as well. Group services were developed to assist students whose problems were largely in the area of interpersonal relations. Also, consultation services were developed with the goals of fostering a campus-wide atmosphere and attitude which allowed for students who received mental health services, if they were at all identifiable, to be treated no differently from other students. Because the clinical cornerstone of the program was to be short-term psychotherapy, procedures for inter-agency referrals were immediately instituted.

Although the proportional representation of specific ethnic groups who have worked in the program has shifted throughout subsequent years, the program's commitment to maintaining a genuinely multiethnic staff has never been challenged or jeopardized. For example, during the academic year 1976-77, there were four senior staff and four trainees, three of whom were Asian, three of whom were White, one of whom was Black, and one of whom was Filipino.

The goal of extending immediate or early appointments to students was consistently met. Rarely did it take more than two days for a student to see a therapist. Emergencies were always given the highest priority and were responded to immediately.

The leave of absence rate for students who have received psychological services has regularly been approximately half the rate of leaves of absence for the general student population. This figure is particularly impressive since students who receive psychological services for the purpose of dealing with personal crises might logically be regarded as having a high-risk potential for dropping out of college, as compared with those students who manage without such services.

The goal of encouraging minority students to utilize psychological services on a proportional basis has been met effectively, with the possible exception of Asian students. Although the intake figures differ from month to month, Black and Hispanic-American students have utilized the program in numbers proportionate to their representation in the student body.

From January 1970 to 1977, over ten thousand individual treatment hours had been provided to almost 4,000 different students.

Based upon the evident success of the "demonstration" project, there was unreserved support for the continuance of the Mental Health Program from students, faculty and administrative staff. Because the "demonstration" purpose of the program had been fulfilled, the Zellerbach Family Fund substantially reduced its funding in 1972. These funds were partially replenished by the Bothin Helping Fund of San Francisco, but in order to restore the program to an adequate level of subsidization, it was necessary to receive subvention from the Community College District.

9

Although the college administration had originally made no firm commitments to allocate funds to the Mental Health Program, the former President of City College, in 1969, expressed in a letter to prospective funding agencies, his confidence that the college could financially support the program through its regular budget, in the event that other sources of funding became unavailabale. That confidence proved to be collectable, for, in 1972, the Community College District allocated $30,000 to insure the continuity of the program. With this allocation, the college became the principal source of funding for the Mental Health Program.

In 1973, the sponsorship of the Mental Health Program was transferred to Progress Foundation, a private non-profit organization which specialized in the administration of half-way facilities for the emotionally disturbed in San Francisco. Each year, from 1973 through 1976, one-year contracts were negotiated between the college district and Progress Foundation, under which the latter organization would provide accountant services, administrative sponsorship, program evaluation and regular psychiatric consultation to the clinical staff by the Medical Director of Progress Foundation).

The end of the academic year 1975-76 marked the culmination and resolution of an impasse which had existed between the Mental Health Program and the college administration. Despite the generous financial support which the program received from the college, the administrative policy of funding the program on a one-year, contractual basis under the auspices of private agencies, was a source of deep insecurity to the staff of the program. Under that administrative arrangement the staff had no assurance, from one year to the next, that they would return to work in September of the forthcoming academic year. Each Spring the staff would anxiously await a resolution from the City College Board of Governors to refund and renegotiate a contract to continue the program.

Because of the perennial tenuousness of the program, the staff recommended to the college administration and Board of Governors that the college permanently integrate the Mental Health Program by allocating funds for two certificated mental health counselor positions. The college administration initially proposed and advocated an alternative measure which would indefinitely integrate the Mental Health Program into the system of the San Francisco Community Mental Health Services (SFCMHS). The college administration had long regarded SFCMHS as the logical inheritor of the Mental Health Program, since there had been a close and harmonious relationship between that agency and the college. The staff of the Mental Health Program, however, considered the college administration's proposal to be fraught

10

with serious pitfalls which would imperil the future of the
program. Basically, the staff regarded the proposal as a measure
which would serve to reinforce the status of the program as an
impermanent service administered by "outsiders." (SFCMHS could
make no financial commitments to the Mental Health Program;
therefore, it was offering only the administrative umbrella of
yet another community agency). The staff believed that permanent
integration of the Mental Health Program into the Student Health
Service was an absolute requisite to the legitimization of the
program as an integral part of the college.

In the Spring 1976, the college administration agreed to
support the principle of a permanently integrated, college-
administered Mental Health Program. Two full-time college-
certificated mental health counselor positions were ratified by
the Board of Governors in the Summer of 1976. Currently (1985),
there are four salaried clinical positions assigned to the Mental
Health Program. The evolution of the program, from a rather
tenuous pilot project to a permanent and integral component of
the college, has been uneven, struggle-ridden and, at times,
painfully slow. However, in an era when mental health services
were generally being defunded and retrenched, the growth and
achievements of the Mental Health Program, made often against
great odds, were truly remarkable.

The process of integrating a mental health program into the
institution of a college might be likened to the transplantation
of a vital organ into the human organism. As in the case of a
dramatic surgical procedure, the expected social responses to a
new mental health service may range from delirious hopes for a
miraculous cure of all systemic disorders to a morbid dread that
the new component will spell death to other components of the
host organism (institution). Very likely, the initial
"organismic" response of the host institution to the introduction
of a mental health program will, at times, be rather allergic
or rejective. The college mental health service, as it is being
newly incorporated into the institutional system, will perhaps be
tainted with a good degree of controversy. Those who work in
such programs should expect that their unconventional presence
will arouse both realistic and unrealistic hopes and suspicions,
in administrators, faculty members and students. These
expectations, whether realistic or not, must be acknowledged with
sensitivity, compassion and respect.

REFERENCES

Allen, N. Physical Culture in Amherst College. Massachusetts:
Stone and Huse, 1869.

Binger, C. A. L. Emotional Disturbances Among College Women.

11

Emotional Problems of the Student. Edited by G. B. Blaine, Jr., and C. C. McArthur. New York: Appleton-Century-Crofts, Inc., 1961.

Carey, J., and Rogers, E. L. Health Status and Health Knowledge of the Student in the Changing Community College. American Journal of Public Health, Vol. 62, No. 2, 1973, 126-133.

Carey, J., Swartz, J., and Leavitt, A. Developing a Mental Health Program at an Urban Community College. Journal of the American College Health Association, 19:200, June 1971, 289-292.

Farnsworth, D. (Ed.) Mental Health in College and University. Cambridge, Mass.: Harvard University Press, 1957.

Farnsworth, D. Psychiatry, Education, and the Young Adult. Illinois: Charles C. Thomas, 1966.

Farnsworth, D. College and Health Administration. New York: Appleton-Century-Crofts, Inc., 1964.

Freedman, M. The College Experience. San Francisco, CA: Jossey-Bass, Inc., 1967.

Wong, J.S. Fifth Chinese Daughter. New York: Harper and Row, 1945.

12

II

HEALTH STATUS AND HEALTH KNOWLEDGE OF THE STUDENT

IN THE CHANGING COMMUNITY COLLEGE

Judith Carey, E. Lance Rogers

This study came about as the direct result of the dearth of factual information concerning the health status of community college students and those students' knowledge of health facilities available to them in college and in the community. While some information concerning the population as a whole and of the four-year college student is available, little is known in these two important areas of the student in the fastest growing segment of higher education -- the community college.

As society has become ever more urbanized, as technology and the economy have grown exponentially, the opportunity in education, especially post-high school education, has become a larger and more important key to American concerns and aspirations. Higher education is thus in an ever increasing stressful position between increasing need and demand, but, proportionately less resources. Accountability being a key which may well increase rather than decrease resources, this study seeks to focus attention on the health status and knowledge of the community college student so that those needs may be properly assessed. From such information, knowledgeable commitment may follow. As needs advance and change, so must the response.

The authors perceived the need for a study of the health status of the students at City College of San Francisco. Moreover, the level of the students' knowledge concerning the health facilities and services available to them and the degree to which the students make use of these facilities and services had not been researched. A questionnaire was prepared, repeatedly pilot-tested and reworked, administered to a suitable sample of our students, and the results analyzed.

Reprinted with permission from the American Journal of Public Health, February, 1977, Vol. 63, No. 2.

Questionnaire

In order to increase the veracity of the answers, the respondents were requested **not** to identify themselves in any way. The questionnaire was of necessity limited in size, and was finally reduced to forty-one significant items. Questions were asked covering such statistical material as age, sex, race, marital status, length of attendance at City College, length of residence in San Francisco, mobility in housing, incidence of certain diseases, coverage by health insurance, coverage by certain welfare programs, the respondent's medical history, use of various drugs and degree of addiction (if applicable), venereal disease history, birth control methods, suicide, emotional crisis, number of children, living accommodations, and use of City College's Student Health Service.

Sample and Methodology

The questionnaire was administered to more than 1,500 students in the health education classes and in the Economic Opportunities Program at City College of San Francisco. The resulting questionnaires were processed and a master deck with each student's response was produced. Using this master record, various item analyses and multivariate analyses were performed to yield results some of which are here reported.

The characteristics of the persons in the sample were checked against known data of our entire student population. The sample proved to correspond quite closely to the mix of the entire student body on the standard variables such as age, sex, wealth, and race. When statements in this report are made concerning the student body as a whole, the necessary slight statistical adjustment has been made to bring the sample into precise correspondence to the available data of the student body as a whole. Whenever the percentages do not add up to 100 per cent for all categories, unless statements are made to the contrary, the reader may interpret the remainder as being accounted for by those who omitted the question. Some of the results of this study follow.

Residence

The students tend to have lived in the same place as they now reside for five years or more. Reference to Table 1 also indicates that women students tend to be slightly less mobile than their male counterparts, but not significantly so.

Length of residence in San Francisco is shown in Table 2.

14

Five years or more of residence was claimed by 76.1 per cent of the men and 80.0 per cent of the women. Only 3.2 per cent indicated they were not residents of San Francisco.

This stability of population is even more remarkable when one remembers that on average, Americans move approximately once in three years.

Morbidity

Table 3 presents the students' answers to a series of questions inquiring if they have or ever had a specific problem. The percentages shown are not low by any usual standard. From the public health viewpoint, the student body of City College of San Francisco is a high-risk population.

Thirty-one-and-a-half per cent of the sample indicated that they have, or have had, at least one of the diseases mentioned in Table 3. When extrapolated to our total day school population this would mean that approximately 4,300 students have, or have had, at least one these diseases.

The Student Health Service at City College reports a maximum of 20 per cent of our students as having some chronic problem on file. Since the percentage found by this study is considerably larger, credence might be given to the theory that much disease is not reported voluntarily in the student's record.

If Illness Strikes

If confronted with sudden illness, 18.6 per cent of the students indicated that they would seek the aid of a private physician. A slightly larger percentage (20.0) of the women fall into this category than do the men (17.6). Approximately 23 per cent of our students indicated they would seek aid from a hospital clinic in an emergency (with no significant variation with sex). The choice of a hospital clinic is not a realistic one. Unless the student were a registered patient, he or she would have to go through an intake procedure and wait approximately three weeks for an appointment for medical care. They might be referred elsewhere, again not a realistic choice. Over 9 per cent of the men and 5 per cent of the women said they would go to a free clinic. This might be a realistic choice as some of these clinics will give immediate attention to a drop-in patient -- some without geographical or eligibility requirement - -but generally these clinics are open only on a limited time schedule which may not coincide with the onslaught of the sudden illness. To seek aid for sudden illness, approximately 46 per cent of the students indicated they would go to an emergency

15

Table 1 - Per cent of Students by Length of Residence in Present
           Domicile

Length of stay	All Students	Male	Female
Less than 6 months	10.3	11.3	9.2
6 months -- less than 1 year	6.5	6.5	6.5
1 year -- less than 2 years	10.3	9.6	10.6
2 years -- less than 5 years	15.2	17.4	13.5
5 years or more	57.7	54.8	59.9

Table 2 - Percentage of Students by Years of Residence in San
          Francisco

Length of residence	All Students	Male	Female
One year or less	6.4	7.5	5.1
Two years	4.4	5.3	3.3
Three Years	4.1	4.2	3.9
Four Years	4.2	3.8	4.6
Five years or more	77.9	76.1	80.0
Not resident or not responding	3.2	3.2	3.1

hospital.

Table 3 -- Morbidity Rates Among Students. Percentages Admitting
Incidence of Problems

Disease or condition	All Students	Male	Female
Tuberculosis	3.6	3.5	3.8
Epilepsy	1.7	1.7	1.7
Diabetes	1.2	1.5	0.8
Heart trouble	3.6	3.8	3.2
Hepititis or infectious mononucleosis	4.3	3.7	5.4
Nervous breakdown	3.8	3.7	3.9
Major surgery	13.9	14.5	13.2
Major orthopedic problems	6.7	9.1	4.2

Of significance is the information that 4 per cent of the
men and 2.8 per cent of the women indicated they would do nothing
if they became suddenly ill and did not have their own private
physician to call. Further analysis of the responses reveals
that the financially poor students (less than $166 monthly salary
per family unit) are more likely to do nothing about their
illness than their richer peers. The rich and poor students are
equally likely to seek help from a private physician. As might
be anticipated, more of the financially disadvantaged students
indicated they would seek aid from free clinics. Approximately
19 per cent of the males with total incomes less than $166 per
month indicated they would go to a free clinic, while those in
the $701 per month and above per family unit indicated the
likelihood of such action to be about one-third of the former
percentage.

Welfare Payments

Table 4 displays the percentage of our students who
acknowledged receipt of full or partial support from the welfare
programs listed. Thus, 24.2 per cent of our students receive
some sort of welfare payment. When extrapolated to the entire
college population this represents about 3,100 students of the
the college population who are receiving some type of welfare
payment.

17

Table 4 -- Percentage of Students Acknowledging Support from
          Various Welfare Programs

Program	All Students	Male	Female
General Assistance	9.6	10.1	9.0
Aid to Families with Dependent Children	10.7	10.8	10.6
Aid to the Needy Blind	1.0	1.0	1.1
Aid to the Totally Disabled	1.0	1.5	0.6
Old Age Assistance	1.9	2.8	1.1

Health Insurance

The current health insurance policy coverage of the students
is shown in Table 5. There are no significant differences in the
responses to this question by sex.

Of the 193 persons who said they were on Aid to Families
with Dependent Children, Aid to the Needy Blind, Aid to the
Totally Disabled, and Old Age Assistance, only 49 stated that
they were covered by "another health insurance policy." Another
55 respondents in the same group said they were not covered by
any health insurance policy. Yet both the group of 49 and the
group of 55 were covered under the program they checked in the
group of four welfare programs indicated above. This would tend
to prove that the students, like many other people, did not know
the extent of their coverage through Medi-Cal and other programs.
On the other hand, excluding those who did not answer the
question, this data indicated that in excess of 3,900 of the
students do not have health insurance or don't know.

18

Table 5 -- Percentages of Students Currently Covered by a
Health Insurance Policy

Coverage	All Students	Male	Female
Blue Cross or CPS	27.0	28.1	24.9
Kaiser Plan	17.5	16.4	19.0
Covered by another policy	24.7	24.6	24.9
Don't know	13.8	14.0	13.3
Not covered by any policy	15.7	15.0	16.9

Sudden Illness

The students were asked to state what mode of transportation
they would use to get to the hospital or doctor's office or
clinic if they became suddenly ill. Their answers are displayed
in Table 6. The reality of their getting to medical aid by bus
or street car when they are ill is not very great. Nor should we
fail to note the 4.3 per cent who admit they would not know what
to do.

Another question was directed toward realism in decision
making. Twelve per cent of the men and 7 per cent of the women
expressed the opinion that if they were hospitalized for a
serious accident or illness for two weeks, it would be necessary
for them to drop out of school. For men, the likelihood of their
saying that they would drop out decreases with age. The self-
predicted drop-out rate for women students is much lower than for
men and is relatively constant throughout the age spectrum. The
male (other than Spanish-speaking) Caucasian is the most likely
to predict drop-out for himself under the stipulated absence for
two weeks due to illness. Since such an absence might perhaps
require a reduction in academic load but should not result in
withdrawal, the need for more intensive advice concerning
educational decisions and the need for more rational choice seem
to be indicated. Perhaps, on the contrary, positive emphasis
should be placed on the 93 per cent of the women students and the
88 per cent of the men who made rational decisions.

19

Table 6 -- Choice of Transportation to Reach Medical Aid if
Sudden Illness Should Strike

Transportation	All Students	Male	Female
Private car	50.0	53.7	46.9
Taxi	18.8	17.1	20.1
Municipal bus or street car	12.0	12.5	11.3
Ambulance	13.5	12.0	15.1
Wouldn´t know what to do	4.3	3.5	5.1

Prescriptions

The action choices of the students if, in the last three
years a doctor prescribed medicine for them, is shown in Table 7.
Of particular significance is the number who did not get their
prescriptions filled because of lack of money. By cross-
reference to other questions it was concluded that 20 percent of
the students do not normally consult with a medical person during
a given year.

Table 7 -- Action of Students when a Doctor Prescribed Medicine
for them

Action	Male	Female
Have the prescription filled and not use it	5.0	3.3
Have the prescription filled and use it	62.8	73.1
Not have the prescription filled because of lack of money	3.3	3.8
Not have the prescription filled because it was not important	1.7	1.0
Not have the prescription filled because you get better	6.3	5.6

20

Weight Problems

Seven and three-tenths per cent of the men and 5.8 per cent of the women indicated that they had been advised by a medical person within the last year that they were underweight. Eight and six-tenths per cent of the men and 16.1 per cent of the women indicated that they had been advised by a medical person within the last year that they were overweight. Fifty-five and one half per cent of the men and 52.8 per cent of the women indicated no weight problem.

Drug Problems

The proportion of students who use drugs and the level of use are shown in Table 8. It is worthwhile to study this table well. Sixty-three and one half per cent of the men and 72.1 per cent of the women stated that they never use drugs. From comparison with the figure given for marijuana one must conclude, with relatively little surprise, that some of the students do not believe that marijuana is a drug.

Twenty-one and six-tenths per cent of the men and 17.4 per cent of the women reported they never had a bad drug trip. Of the men, 9.6 per cent reported they had a bad drug trip and just let it take care of itself, while only 5.3 per cent of the women reported similarly. One and seven-tenths per cent of the men reported they called on someone for help when they had a bad drug trip, while 3.1 per cent of the women reported similarly. Only 1.8 per cent of the men and 0.8 per cent of the women reported they went to a medical facility for help when they had a bad drug trip that really scared them. Again, 1.8 per cent of the men and 1.4 per cent of the women reported that they had taken medication to counteract the bad trip. Forty and eight-tenths per cent of the men and 37.9 per cent of the women who said they were on drugs admitted that they had had a bad trip. Among the students, as elsewhere, the user of drugs is very much alone.

The level of drug usage is clearly shown in Table 8. So that the reader may appreciate the magnitude of the problem, some of the percentages have been extrapolated to the entire student body. Thus, 1,110 of the students at City College claim to have used amphetamines (speed, crystals, dexies, pep pills, bennies, uppers, sunshines) more than 10 times. Thus, 390 male students have used acid more than 30 times. There are 240 students using hard narcotics daily. Use of drugs, especially among men, is significant.

21

Table 8 -- Percentages of Students Using Drugs

Marijuana	Male	Female	Amphetamines	Male	Female
Never	45.7	56.9	Never	70.6	78.3
Once only	13.1	12.4	Once only	6.5	4.6
Once a month	11.1	11.7	2-5 times	7.3	6.1
Weekly	16.4	13.5	5-10 times	2.3	2.4
Daily	11.3	2.9	More than 10 times	11.0	6.3

Psychedelics	Male	Female	Hard narcotics	Male	Female
Never	76.6	86.7	Never	83.6	90.7
Once only	4.7	3.5	Once only	2.8	2.8
2-10 times	6.8	4.9	Twice	7.3	3.2
10-30 times	3.2	1.3	Two times a week	0.7	0.1
More than 30 times	6.5	1.5	Daily	3.0	0.8

Venereal Disease

The students were asked to designate the place where they were treated if they had contracted venereal disease. These results are shown in Table 9. Extrapolated to the total college population at City College, 70 students admitted to having contracted venereal disease and "gone without treatment." The admitted incidence rate of venereal disease among men was almost twice as large as that among women.

The pattern of venereal disease incidence as indicated by the responses, shows that for the males the rate is less than average for the 18-, 19- and 20-year old but greater than average for the older males. For example, of the 21- or 22-year old group, only 61.0 per cent have never had venereal disease. For the women in the same group the rate is 60.7 per cent. However, the rate remains approximately 61 per cent for the males for all older groups whereas the rate jumps to 90.9 per cent for the 23- and 24-year old women and to 79.3 per cent for the 27-year-old

22

and over group of women. Of significance is the increased reliance on the private physician and the free clinic as the student becomes older. No woman reports either using "other treatments" or going without treatment after 20 years of age. For the men, the tendency to neglect or not properly care for oneself persists to age 24. Seven and three-tenths per cent of the men in the 21- or 22-year -old group reported using "other methods of treatment" for venereal disease and 2.4 per cent of this group reported going without treatment. For the 23- and 24-year-old group the corresponding percentages are 5.7 and zero. Both percentages are zero for the 27 years and over group. There was no significant correlation with race in the statistics dealing with the incidence of venereal disease.

Table 9 -- If Students Had Contracted Venereal Disease, Where Did They Seek Treatment?

Treated at	Male	Female
Private physician´s office	6.5	5.8
Free or low cost clinic	6.5	2.6
Other means of treatment	2.7	0.1
Go without treatment	0.8	0.3
Never had venereal disease	76.4	83.1

Sexual Problems

The responses of the students to the question "are you ever worried by sexual problems" is displayed in Table 10.

Those who said they were worried "all of the time" correlated positively with the very poor and the very rich, and negatively with those in the middle monthly income brackets. Apparently the very rich (more than $701 monthly income and the very poor (less than $166 monthly income) were more concerned with sexual problems than were those between these extremes of monthly income. Further analysis shows that the Orientals rate themselves as being worried "all of the time" about sexual matters less than average, the Caucasians (Spanish surname) are at the average of all students, while the Black and the Caucasian (other than Spanish surname), rate themselves as being in this category more than average.

23

Table 10 -- Frequency of Worry Over Sexual Problems

Frequency	Male	Female
Never	40.5	39.4
Seldom	23.6	22.6
Sometimes	25.1	29.2
Often	4.2	3.1
All the time	4.5	2.2

Pregnancy and Abortion

The students were asked what they would do if they were female, unmarried, and pregnant. The responses are shown in the Table 11.

Eighty-six and three-tenths per cent of the Black women students said they would have the baby and keep him/her. Sixty per cent of the Spanish surname Caucasians, 53.3 per cent of the other Caucasians (non-Spanish surname, and 53 per cent of the Orientals responded similarly. None of the Black women students said they would have the baby and arrange for an adoption, but 6.9 per cent of the Spanish surname Caucasians, 12.3 per cent of the other Caucasian, and 12.6 per cent of the Oriental women students said they would. Nine per cent of the Black women students said they would have a legal therapeutic abortion. However, 21.5 per cent of the Oriental, 24.5 per cent of the Spanish surname Caucasian, and 32.0 per cent of the other Caucasian women said they would.

None of the Spanish surname Caucasian women students would have an illegal abortion, but 0.9 per cent of the Black, 1.6 per cent of the other Caucasian, and 1.9 per cent of the Oriental women said they would. Nine-tenths of one per cent of the Black women students said they would attempt self-abortion, while 2.3 per cent of the Oriental, 3.0 per cent of the Spanish surname Caucasian, and 7.4 per cent of the other Caucasian said they would attempt a similar solution.

24

Table 11 -- If You Were Female, Unmarried, and Pregnant, What Would You Do?

Proposed solution	Male	Female
Have the baby and keep him/her	30.7	57.1
Have the baby and adopt him/her out	7.3	9.6
Have a legal therapeutic abortion	14.6	23.9
Have an illegal abortion	2.8	1.4
Use home remedy (attempt self-abortion)	2.3	1.3

Birth Control

The students were asked what method of birth control they preferred. Their responses are shown in Table 12.

Fifty-five and four-tenths per cent of the Caucasian (other than Spanish surname) women indicated they were in favor of using the pill. The remainder of the racial groups in descending order of their likelihood of using the pill are as follows: Black (46.0), Spanish (44.2), Oriental (27.2), other (29.6). Similarly ranked according to the likelihood of their using chemical means of birth control, the groups and their percentages are: Black (9.0), other (4.5), Spanish surname (2.1), Oriental (2.8), and other Caucasian (2.0). Ranked according to their likelihood of using mechanical methods of birth control, the groups and their percentages are: other (22.6), Oriental 13.6, other Caucasian (13.2), Spanish surname (10.8), Black (9.9). Ranked according to their proneness to use home remedy as a birth control measure, the groups are: Black (1.8), other Caucasian (0.8) and all the other groups are zero. Ranked acccording to their likelihood of using no birth control or having never thought about it, the groups and their percentages are: Oriental (53.7), Spanish (39.2), other (36.4), Black (30.7), other Caucasian (24.6).

Table 12 -- Students´ Preference as to Method of Birth Control

Method	Male	Female
"The pill"	34.2	42.5
Chemical means	2.7	3.6
Mechanical means	12.0	12.9
Home remedy	2.7	0.6
None or never thought about it	25.4	36.8

Suicide

The students´ replies to being asked what they did if they ever seriously thought about committing suicide are recorded in Table 13.

Extrapolated to the entire student body, approximately 440 persons, both male and female, said that they had attempted suicide. There was no significant correlation between wealth as measured by monthly income and suicide proneness. Projecting to our college (day) student population, there are perhaps 3,900 students on campus who say that they have thought seriously about committing suicide.

Table 13 -- Students´ Replies to Being Asked What They Did If They Ever Seriously Thought About Committing Suicide

Alternatives	Male	Female
Seek help and, or, tell anyone	5.8	5.3
Decide you didn´t have the guts to do and forget it	8.8	16.1
Attempt suicide	2.7	3.9
Do nothing about it, just keep thinking about it	11.5	10.6
Never thought about it	63.0	60.4

26

Severe Emotional Crisis

The students were asked what they did if they had a severe emotional upset or crisis. Eighteen and nine-tenths per cent of the men and 32.6 per cent of the women responded that they sought help from family or friends. However, 5.5 per cent of the men and 6.3 per cent of the women said they had sought professional help. Fourteen and one-tenth per cent of the men and 11.7 per cent of the women said they did nothing about it. Forty-eight and seven-tenths per cent of the men and 39.7 per cent of the women reported they never had a severe emotional upset. These statistics appear to indicate a group in greater need of help than is usually reported in college populations.

Children Under Five

In an effort to determine how great a need there might be for child care assistance for our students, the respondents were asked about their dependents. Based on their responses, there appears to be approximately 5,000 children under five years of age living with our students and for whom the students are responsible. This is about one-third of the student population.

Summary

Results of a study concerning the health status of community college students and those students' knowledge of health facilities available to them in college and in the community is reported. A representative sample of more than 1.500 students at City College of San Francisco answered a 41-item questionnaire. Information was obtained on a wide spectrum of problems and issues of importance in understanding and helping the community college student including: residence, mobility, age, sex, race, wealth, incidence of certain diseases, health insurance coverage, welfare coverage, drug usage, venereal disease history, preferred birth control methods, suicide tendencies, and number of dependent children. The primary purpose of this study was not to provide answers or to estimate the students' self-response interpretation of questions but to attempt to evaluate how the students perceive their health needs and status and what actions they would take under certain conditions. Results indicate the student body to be a high-risk population from the public health viewpoint. The students showed a higher prevalence of health needs than was initially suspected and decreased ability to deal realistically with those needs.

27

III

THE PAUCITY OF MENTAL HEALTH SERVICES AND

PROGRAMS IN COMMUNITY COLLEGES:

IMPLICATIONS OF A SURVEY

GERALD AMADA

The experience of organizing and implementing a community college psychological service stimulated interest in gaining an overview of the extent and nature of mental health services throughout the entire community college system in California, with obvious implications on a national scale.

Method

A survey was devised to evaluate current mental health programs on California's commmunity college campuses. The survey was initially conducted by mailing questionnaires to all public and private community colleges listed in the California Junior College Association Directory; a total of exactly 100 schools. Fifty-one of these schools responded to the written questionnaire. By undertaking telephonic contacts with the remaining schools a 100 per cent response to the questionnaire was achieved.

Although the mailings were addressed to the college dean of students, responses were provided by a wide variety of knowledgeable and authoritative college representatives, including deans, nurses, counselors, health officers and psychotherapists. Respondents were asked the following questions:

1. Are mental health or psychological services offered on your campus?

Reprinted with permission from the Journal of American College Health, Vol. 23, No. 5, June 1975.

2. If such services are offered, could you describe the extent of these services?

3. If mental health services are not offered, do you think there is an appreciable need for such services on your campus?

4. Are psychologically oriented services provided by the academic counseling department on your campus?

5. If psychologically oriented services are offered on your campus, roughly what percentage of counseling service time is devoted to intensive psychological intervention or psychotherapy?

6. Is there an official policy in relation to having the counseling or any other department provide psychotherapy to students?

7. Please indicate the level of enrollment, including day and evening students.

8. In what manner and by what departmental service are psychiatric emergencies (i.e., uncontrollable or severe drug and psychotic reactions) coped with?

9. Is there a campus service which provides psychiatric medications?

10. If there is no campus service which provides psychiatric medications, do you think that there is an apppreciable need for establishing such a service?

11. If mental health services are provided on your campus, what is their source of funding?

12. Is consultation, with respect to the psychological needs of students, provided to the college faculty and administrative personnel?

13. If such consultation is not available, do you think there is an appreciable need for such a service on your campus?

Results

1. Are Services Offered. In response to this question, 62% of the community colleges indicated that they did not offer mental health or psychological services on campus.

2. Extent of Services. Thirty-eight community colleges provide mental health services, ranging from two to ninety hours per week. The average number of hours of psychological services provided by these programs was twenty-seven per week. The total number of service hours for all 100 colleges was 1,010 per week.

3. Need for Services. Of the sixty-two community colleges which do not provide mental health services, 53 or 85%, responded "Yes" to this question.

4. Psychologically Oriented Services. In response to this question 52% of the schools responded "Yes."

5. Percentage of Counseling Time. Representatives at six of the fifty-two schools in which counselors devote some percentage of their time to psychologically oriented services refused to estimate the percentage of time counselors devote to this activity, other than to indicate that such assistance to students was "minimal." At the forty-six other schools the estimated range of time devoted to this type of service was from 1% to 50%; the average for all forty-six schools was 23%.

6. Official Policies. In response to this question, 90% of the schools replied "NO." Of the ten schools which replied "Yes," eight stated that there was a policy which prohibited counselors from providing pscyhotherapy. Two schools indicated there was an official policy in favor of an on-campus psychotherapeutic service.

7. Enrollment Figures. The enrollment figures ranged from a low of 250 to a high of 31,461 day and evening students per college. Total enrollment for all California community colleges, excluding City College of San Francisco, is approximately 780,000 students (1975).

8. Psychiatric Emergencies. In response to this question, all 100 colleges responded similarly. Psychiatric emergencies were generally referred to the person on campus who was regarded to be officially responsible for, or most knowledgeable, in handling such matters. If the emergency required service off-campus, the college then arranged for transportation to a community psychiatric facility. In most such instances attempts were made to enlist the assistance of potentially helpful persons, such as family members, police and ambulance service personnel. No community college reported maintaining a campus facility which provided round-the-clock, physically secure care for students who required this kind of service.

9. Medications. In response to this question, 91% of the

31

schools indicated that there was no campus service which provided psychiatric medications.

10. Need for Psychiatric Medications. Of the 91 schools which did not provide psychiatric medications, one indicated uncertainty as to need, 36 indicated no appreciable need and 54 or 59% indicated an appreciable need for this modality of service.

11. The following is a breakdown of funding sources for the 38 schools which did provide on-campus mental health services.

Table I

Source of Funding	Number of Schools
District Funding	18
Student Health Fee	11
County Funding	3
State Funding	2
Privately Donated Services	1
Joint District and County Funding	1
Joint District Funding and Privately Donated Services	1
Joint District Funding and Student Health Fee	1
	N = 38

12. Consultation. In response to this question, 54% of the community colleges indicated that they did not provide consultation to the faculty and administration with respect to the psychological needs of students.

13. Need for Consultation. Of the 54 schools which did not provide consultation, 48 or 89% indicated that an appreciable need existed for such a college service.

Discussion

The fact that almost two-thirds of California's community colleges do not provide on-campus mental health services in itself invites further study. This figure, coupled with the findings that 85% of those schools which lack these services also indicate an appreciable need for on-campus mental health services, further dramatizes a glaring gap in the educational system. Another way of viewing this issue is to consider full-time mental health positions in terms of 40 hours a week of service and convert into full-time positions the total number of mental health service hours per week provided collectively by all of the states community colleges (1,010 hours). By doing this we discover that there are only 25 "full-time" mental health positions on all of California's community college campuses. The ratio of campus psychotherapists to the 780,000 community college students throughout the state is approximately one psychotherapist for every 31,200 students!

Two factors are often adduced in an attempt to minimize the significance of community college mental health services. Firstly, it has been argued, that college counselors capably meet the psychological needs of students. That this is not the case has no bearing on the qualifications or competency of college counselors. In fact, most seem to provide highly effective counseling services.

Nevertheless, academic counseling is not psychotherapy. Psychotherapy requires a different (not better) set and range of professional skills and techniques. This has been implicitly recognized in the California educational codes which state that "counseling services shall assist each student in the college in the following ways: (a) to determine his educational goals, and (b) to make a self-appraisal toward his goals (California Community Colleges, 1970). Although psychotherapeutic services often incorporate these educational objectives, the goals of psychotherapy are frequently broader or depart, to some extent, from immediate educational considerations. In any case, although psychologically oriented work is undertaken by counselors at 52% of the community colleges in this study, the average percentage of time devoted to such intervention is only 23%. Furthermore, most of the 52 schools which provide psychologically oriented counseling services, readily acknowledge that although these services are often intensive, they should not be deemed psychotherapy.

Other objections sometimes raised against on-campus mental health services relate to low student enrollment and the availability of community psychiatric facilities. In some instances small student populations appear not to warrant on-campus psychological services. In other instances, the ready availability and physical propinquity of community psychiatric services would appear to render an on-campus mental health program ineffectual and a duplication of community services. Despite these possible objections to on-campus psychological services, it is clearly significant that of the 62 schools without these programs, 53 or 85% reported the need for them.

33

The results presented in Table II indicate, as expected, that those schools with larger student populations (over 10,000 students) tend to provide on-campus mental health services more often than those schools with smaller student populations (under 10,000 students).

Table II

Schools Offering Mental Health Services

Size of Enrollment	Yes	No
0- 4,999	6	23
5.000- 9.999	8	20
10,000-14,999	9	6
15,000-19,999	12	9
20,000-24,999	2	1
25,000-29,999	0	2
30,000-34,999	1	1
	N = 38	N = 62

The data presented in Table III suggest that an appreciable need for an on-campus mental health service does not necessarily reflect a large student population. Although the largest number of colleges which indicated no appreciable need for mental health services had enrollments under 5,000 students, 16, or about 70% of those schools with enrollments below 5,000 students, indicated an appreciable need for these programs. The fact that size of enrollment does have some bearing on the need for psychological services is demonstrated, however, by the finding that 37, or about 95% of the 39 schools which lack on-campus psychological services and have enrollments over 5,000 students, indicated the need for these services.

The finding that 90% of the community colleges lacked an official policy with respect to the delivery of on-campus mental health services, suggests that such services could be relatively easily instituted and implemented on those campuses which lacked them, providing that adequate funds and physical facilities were made available.

34

Table III

Schools Expressing Appreciable Need

For Mental Health Services

Size of Enrollment	Yes	No
0- 4,999	16	7
5,000- 9,999	20	0
10,000-14,999	5	1
15,000-19,999	8	1
20,000-24,999	1	0
25,000-29,999	2	0
30,000-34,999	1	0
	N=53	N=9

Although all the community colleges had an established procedure for coping with psychiatric emergencies, the absence of round-the-clock, physically secure and carefully supervised facilities for students in crisis raises important questions. How much less stigmatizing would protective care in a campus facility be than in a community psychiatric hospital? What are the potentially harmful effects which result from the delays, public exposure and clamor which ordinarily accompany psychiatric hospitalization in the community? Many universities have developed 24-hour infirmary facilities in response to just such considerations. It may be necessary for the community colleges to follow suit.

It is significant that 54 or 59% of the 91 schools which do not maintain programs which provide psychiatric medications, indicated an appreciable need for this modality of service. This figure demonstrates the need amongst these schools to investigate opportunities for funding, medical supervision and licensure and developing physical facilities for the safe impoundment of psychiatric medications. If these conditions can be met, it is apparent that psychiatric drugs can be a timely and helpful treatment modality, particularly when used in conjunction with ongoing psychotherapy.

The figures in Table I indicate that 18 or 47% and 11 or 29%

35

of the schools with mental health services received funding for these programs from the college district and student health fees respectively. The lack of uniformity in the funding sources of community college mental health programs reflects the necessity of each college to generate its own funds in order to subsidize these services. Faced with this dilemma, the colleges have either failed to establish the programs at all or have generated funds according to the particular financial resources and limitations of the college. Viewed from a statewide perspective this form of individualism has resulted in a patently inequitable, chaotic and inefficacious system of funding community college mental health programs. Figures in Table I additionally indicate that 74% of California´s community college mental health programs are subsidized exlusively by college district funds.

The data provided in Table IV indicate that programs financed by college districts tend to provide more hours of psychological service than programs subsidized by other sources. The fact that such a widespread precedent for this use of district funding already exists, suggests that the likelihood that those 53 community colleges which indicate an appreciable need for on-campus mental health services would readily institute psychological services if adequate funds for these programs became available to the various school districts.

The finding that 89% of the community colleges which lack psychological consultation indicate an appreciable need for such a resource is noteworthy. The potential value of psychological consultation was highlighted by many college officials who reported faculty and administrators frequently felt alarmed or confused over how to cope with emotionally disturbed students.

36

Table IV

Weekly Hours	of	Psychological		Service
Source of Funding	0-19	20-39	40-59	60-79	80-99
District Funds	4	4	8		2
Health Fee	6	3	2		
County Funds	2		1		
State Funds	2				
Joint District Funding and Health Fee				1	
Joint District Funding and Privately Donated Service		1			
Joint District and County Funds	1				
Privately Donated Services	1				
Totals	16	8	11	1	2

N-38

The findings of this survey have implications which reach far beyond the borders of California. If we can justifiably assume that the colleges included in this survey are relatively representative of other community colleges in the nation, there then seems cause for carefully evaluating the status of mental health services on all community college campuses throughout the country. The urgency for such studies must be recognized because "while most categories of colleges and universities are growing in number, by far the greatest increase is in public community colleges. During the 1960´s such schools increased in number from 330 to 650 (97%)" (Glasscote, et al., 1973).

Summary

This survey and most epidemiological studies of college students demonstrate a profound need for on-campus mental health services which can offer psychological assistance immediately, confidentially and intensively. The implications of the survey

37

are national in scope. Such programs demonstrably depend upon the expenditure of considerable funds. Whether mental health services are offered under the campus aegis of the counseling department or student health service probably should be determined by the particular administrative priorities, orientation, resources and limitations of those respective departments. What undoubtedly is required is state and federal legislation which will allocate to community college districts funds for organizing the mental health programs for which they are expressing an apprecialbe need. Only by this means can the psychological needs of community college students receive the recognition and respect to which they are entitled.

REFERENCES

California Community Colleges, State of California, Title 5, Part VI, Register 70, No. 16 (4/18/70), 618.

Glasscote, R., et al. Mental Health on the Campus. Washington, D.C.: Joint Information Services of the American Psychiatric Assocation and the National Association for Mental Health, 1973.

IV

INCREASING BLACK STUDENTS' UTILIZATION

OF MENTAL HEALTH SERVICES

Kenneth Davis, Jacqueline Swartz

For many Black people, going to a mental health service is a
ready admission of being crazy. For Black males, the suggestion
that they are not coping effectively with their lives touches
highly sensitive areas of identity and masculinity. For females,
concern for femininity does not seem to be as much of an issue as
anxiety over not being able to deal adequately with problems,
handle crises, and arrive at appropriate solutions.   Most Black
people do not come in contact with psychiatric clinics unless
overtly disruptive, psychotic, or arrested. Psychiatry is often
viewed as a punitive profession and is frequently associated with
social or medical agencies identified with invasions of privacy
and confidentiality. Then there are the clinics themselves, with
their cumbersome intake   procedures   and   often   derogatory
prerequisites. If treatment is initiated, the therapist will
most likely be white and will probably be viewed as an alien
person unable to   understand   the   personal and   sociological
pressures that are obvious and inescapable to a Black person.
The white therapist might be thought of as part of the white
power structure -- an   authority figure whose orientation and
training will most probably mean a long, tediously analytic
process designed to plug the patient   into his   childhood while
ignoring the basis for supicion and distrust that summon feelings
of impotence, frustration, and anger in Black people.   This is
hardly a milieu for successful therapy. Treatment is complicated
by agencies that often view the patient as resistant, suspicious,
and hostile, while remaining insensitive to what it is that makes
for this reaction.   Black people, who have survived a society
that has denied and delayed possibilities for the fulfillment of
basic human needs, can hardly be expected to be receptive to the

Reprinted with permission from the American Journal of
Orthopsychiatry, Vol. 42, No. 5 (October, 1972).

delayed gratification process that therapy represents. It seems plausible that Blacks often want to focus on the "here and now."

Black people who appear at mental health clinics usually come because of a crisis and are often referred to emergency units offering immediate psychiatric attention. One of my goals as a Black therapist at City College of San Francisco was to see students before they reached the crisis point. This preventive orientation required particular knowledge of Black students and their context at the college.

City College

Fifteen per cent of all registered students at City College take a leave of absence some time during each semester. About 10% re-register after having dropped out of school without completing an earlier semester. In "Minority Group Attrition at City College - A Case Study," Dr. Joseph H. Jacobsen documents that 53% of the Black students entering in 1963 dropped out by the end of the year. In discussing the College's lack of holding power for these students, Dr. Jacobsen concludes that:

> The heart-breaking disappointment, the waste resulting from partially achieved goals and unused capacities, and the potential economic and social problems evident in these cold figures are a challenge to the entire faculty. Surely one of the highest priorities at City College of San Francisco must be given to ways and means of salvaging the educationally disadvantaged Black students.

Among his suggestions are increased tutoring and other kinds of individual attention; more financial assistance through jobs or stipends; more intensive counseling; encouragement through close relationships with faculty; and an orientation at City College more in keeping with student needs.

In working positively with Black students, the faculty member, administrator, or helping person should be aware of the multiplicity of problems students face, problems clearly reflected in language and reading skills and chracterized by borderline academic achievement as defined in terms of the white majority culture. In addition, there are problems created by the difference between the ethnic and cultural identity of many students and the milieu of the school in which students spend a block of time on campus with a minimum of social involvement. About the only sizable gathering place is the cafeteria, and the location of the college in a residential area isolated from the main parts of the city precludes the existence of a campus community. Many students are further distanced from campus life

40

by having to work part or full time, often in areas that are miles away from the school.

Like most urban community colleges, City College was established as a post-high school institution designed to serve a homogeneous group of students interested in completing university parallel programs. Today, the students at City College are much more representative of the total San Francisco population, socially, ethnically, culturally, and economically. Sixty per cent are enrolled in university parallel courses, and 40% in vocational progams. The reponse of the college to the changing nature of the student body and the heavy minority representation has been to establish remedial programs. These range from "English As A Second Language" (mainly used by minority students with no knowledge of English) to tutorial services, to a program funded by Senate Bill 164 designed to recruit people from the ghettos, place them in school, and supply them with remedial classes until they are able to enter regular college classes. While these programs might fill educational gaps for people who have deficiencies in basic reading or mathematical skills, they do not serve to motivate or offer a challenge to students whose intelligence has only been turned off by consistently negative school experiences. City College should be aware of those students it has failed to teach and should provide them with a meaningful education. Students from diverse backgrounds often have special knowledge and sensibilities, and these resources could be tapped at the same time that creativity and motivation are demanded. Although ethnic studies could be posed to show a response to the cultural diversity of the student body, ethnic studies occupies a low priority in the school´s curriculum. More important, however, is the predominant institutional attitude, according to which grade point average is not only the measure of success but the motivation for learning. Those students who manage to study often do so for grades only. And those who stay in school but find it difficult or impossible to concentrate usually blame themselves instead of the methods of delivery and the content of the education they are supposed to be receiving. They feel they should make a huge effort, not because of the reward of self-fulfillment, knowledge, or increased awareness, but because good grades and conformity to the teacher´s goals can mean a better job, security, and status -- rewards that come only after a long period of self-denial. This situation exists, of course, in middle-class universities and certainly in graduate school. Students in the large or elite universities have insisted, however, that their education be rewarding and exciting; this demand can be seen from philosophy classes to medical schools. Yet if the quality of education at middle-class institutions has glaring deficiencies, these deficiencies, while perceived less, have even more effect on the community college

41

population described above.

City College students come in large numbers from three Black areas: Hunter's Point, Western Addition, and Ocean-Merced-Ingleside. The vast majority of residents of these areas who attend college are students at City College. There are certain documented or assumed problems in these areas, including low average incomes, high unemployment rates, substandard and crowded housing contributing to family and marital conflict, low education levels, and a high crime rate resulting in numerous arrests. Since the college population comes from these areas, it can only be expected that the students will bring with them the influence of their environment.

Mental Health Services

It was hoped that students would use mental health services in the same racial percentage that they existed in the student body. To encourage this, at least 50% of the mental health staff was from minority groups. Their presence was designed to help minority students feel at ease in coming to the health services. More important than that, of course, is that a minority staff member has a special background and knowledge enabling him to be attuned to the minority student as well as to represent an identity model. The latter is important, since for many students City College provides the last chance or only access to a college education or desirable job skills. In spite of many obstacles, the opportunity is not as quickly discarded if there is a visible model of someone close who has "made it." Furthermore, the model of the minority professional working with people of his own group sets an example contrary to that of the person who, having received training and certification, quickly moves to a middle-class area where the need for him is minimal compared to that in his own community. The program at City College has indeed shown minority staff that working with one's own people can be a successful and rewarding experience, both professionally and personally.

Bringing the Service to the Student

The staff at the student health service was aware that minority students tend to be blocked from utilizing services. Staff members began to investigate innovative ways of bringing the service to these students, keeping in mind the student's own cultural patterns and value systems while trying to maintain the goals of delivering care and improving prevention. As a Black therapist, I was especially concerned with developing new ways of bringing the service to Black students. To do this I used a variety of methods. I arranged for several local public radio

42

stations catering to Blacks to run a continuing blurb on the mental health program at the college. I emphasized, identifying myself by name and giving my on-campus location, that a "brother" was available for individual and group counseling. I stressed some of the problems students were likely to feel, including personal, family, and marital conflicts, and gave tips on how to use the service that were compatible with Black students' identity. I projected a degree of informality and suggested that students drop by the Health Service if only to check out who I was.

Working with the general goal of indirect consultation and the specific one of providing direct service to Black students, I contacted all Black staff in key positions at the college, including the Dean of Men, the chairperson of Afro-American studies, and the campus group advisor. I circulated with various Black faculty and was able to meet many Black students on a personal basis. I felt that students were able to relate to me as a Black person, yet see me as a mental health professional. Reaction was favorable, and succeeding contacts were often made by students on a formal and informal basis around a variety of problems. I also met informally with members of the Black Student Union at their headquarters on campus.

In all of the above efforts, I tried to be visible as a non-faculty professional. In doing so I learned that informality and professionalism can be extremely compatiable and indeed more penetrating than the usual formally structured therapist-client interaction. I went outside the usual process in which the client makes an appointment and is then told when he may be seen at the therapist's office. It was essential to make contact with the students in their own milieu, whether that be the cafeteria (where contact with one student would often generate other contacts), parking lot, or the Black Student Union. Mobility was a key factor in this approach, according to which my visibility as a therapist became the message. Although this method was impossible to evaluate thoroughly, it does indicate that the service can be brought to the student. While this was the primary objective, another goal was reached when students began to drop by the office on an informal or "rap" basis. This was done partially through initial casual contacts around campus, when I would suggest setting aside some time to talk in more detail in my office. Some students were seen on a short-term basis, others for more long-term, ongoing treatment. And there were some who were actually regulars although they never made an appointment. The "open door" policy attracted a number of students, some of whom could only advance to the point of putting one foot in the door. Others came accompanied by a friend who, after an initial introduction, might proceed to make an

43

appointment.

The increase in intake of Black students can be shown over three periods of the 1970 spring semester. From Janaury 1 to March 20, Black students represented 9% of the total intake at the Mental Health Service; from March 20 to May 8, Black intake jumped to 21%; from May 11 to June 12 it rose to 23.6% This increase in intake clearly reflects greater utilization of the service.

The Black students who requested treatment were usually not seriously disturbed, and many had conflicts over concrete problems such as finances, family, nd school. There seemed to be a minimum of focus on the interpersonal problems typical among white students, such as depression and anxiety over leaving home or dating conflicts. The Black students did present identity problems, however, and some felt conflict over being unable to identify with Black militants on campus while believing they ought to give their allegiance to this group. Many students come to the Mental Health Service at a pre-crisis level, and I could speculate that the timing of the intervention had preventive significance. Coupled with the fact that many Black people receive treatment only at a crisis point, I could predict that within the City College population, if there were no intervention prior to crisis, some students would resolve their problems themselves; others would use such means as drugs, drinking, dropping out, and bizarre behavior. Once students were in treatment, most were seen from two to four times; some were seen as many as ten times, however.

Conclusion

One of the most important factors in changing utilization of services was personalized contact. I found that by emphasizing my own visibility through use of informal techniques, I was able to facilitate contact and reach a sizable number of the Black target population. It should be added here that, because of the turnover of the student population in one- or two-year programs, continued outreach efforts have to be maintained. During my year-and-a-half at City College, I was able to make contacts by taking steps out of the ordinary realm of conventional intervention. Certainly any professional who sets out to reach a unique group of clients should tailor his choice of methods to the needs of the target population.

44

V

TRAINING MINORITY MENTAL HEALTH PROFESSIONALS

Alan Leavitt, Andrew Curry

Pilot Mental Health Program

Because of the special nature of the student body and the severe financial limitations placed on student health services, it was clear that unconventional mental health programs would have to be developed for San Francisco City College. One of our first decisions was that at least half the staff members of the newly established mental health program should be from racial minorities. That was compelled by ethical considerations, by the conviction that minority students would feel more comfortable with minority staff, and by the belief that minority staff would have a unique perspective to contribute to the development of a relevant program for minority students (Davis and Swartz, 1972).

Currently (1971) the permanent staff consists of two psychiatric social workers, two psychologists, and two psychiatrists; all but two work part-time. One of the advantages to using part-time workers is that we can get a broader racial distribution than with fewer full-time workers; the staff include two Whites, two Chinese, one Latin, and one Black. In addition, the service is busy only eight months of the year, and it is easier to contract with people for only part of a year if they work on a part-time basis.

Once we recruited minority staff, we began to develop the training program. We found that many Bay Area institutions offering training in the mental health professions had been recruiting minority graduate students and trainees and promising them the opportunity to work with minority and low-income groups. However, administrators were having difficulty delivering on those

Reprinted with permission from Hospital and Community Psychiatry, Vol. 63, No. 2 (August, 1973).

promises. Since we had 7,000 Third World students on campus,
many of whom needed mental health services, City College offered
a unique opportunity for training.   We were convinced that a
first-rate training program   could be developed for minority
trainees, and direct services could be provided simultaneously
for large numbers of students needing treatment.

We asked training directors of various disciplines in those
institutions to consider using our student health service as a
field placement. We had a rapid response, and more trainees than
we could handle. We selected 11. Seven were first-year graduate
students whom we considered beginning trainees because of their
lack of formal psychotherapeutic experience. Two were
registered nurses interested in psychiatric and college health
nursing, two were psychiatric social workers, one was a
vocational rehabilitation counselor, one was a counseling
psychologist, and one was a student with a graduate degree in
experimental psychology.

In addition we had four senior trainees; two were third-year
psychiatric residents, one was a psychiatric social worker in his
fourth year of graduate clinical training, and one was a second-
year student in vocational rehabilitation counseling.   Three of
the 11 trainees were foreign-born and four were White, three
Black, three Chinese, and one Latin. Eight were at the health
service half-time and the other three lesser amounts of time.

The trainees came to the student health service without
expecting any salary. When we realized the severe financial
stress they were under while completing their graduate education,
we secured funds to support their training.   We were able to
offer stipends to the eight half-time trainees. The stipend
enhanced the morale of the trainees and gave concrete evidence of
our respect for and interest in them.

Because the mental health program and the student health
service were expanding rapidly, trainees were in a position to
help design their own training program.   They were involved in
planning many of the new student health programs, including the
liaison services to minority student organizations, and later
participated in planning training conferences, selecting
conference leaders and supervisors, and recruiting new trainees.
The permanent staff, trainees, and students planned and developed
the mental health program from year to year. As the program
developed, senior staff functioned more as supervisors and
consultants, while trainees provided direct services.   That
increased services available to students and provided a
stimulating learning experience for graduate trainees.

46

Crisis treatment is the primary service offered to the largest number of students requesting mental health appointments. Immediate appointments are always available, but a five-session limit is generally established. Long-term individual treatment is not emphasized, except that each trainee is expected to treat several students for extended periods because of the additional learning experience it offers the trainee, and because some students find it beneficial. We encouraged trainees to establish therapy groups during the academic year with seven or eight students and one or two group therapists.

Trainees are also expected to spend one-third of their time outside the health service, primarily as liaisons to students and faculty organizations. For example, a psychiatric nurse who had formerly been a fashion model worked with faculty in the women's physical education department, which offered special classes for obese women. A group of the women met with the nurse weekly. Initially the emphasis was on makeup, dress, and posture. Gradually the discussions shifted to a consideration of the physiological aspects of obesity, and finally to some of the psychological issues inherent in obesity. As the women in the group began to lose weight, there were intensive discussions of changing bodily images and the underlying functions the obesity served.

The Black trainees helped students who were trying to increase the effectiveness of the Black Students' Union. Trainees worked with students to develop new campus activities in which the BSU could be involved. At the same time efforts were directed toward increasing the BSU membership andl locating and decorating a permanent office for the organization. The office ultimately became a social center for a significant number of Black students when they had free time on campus. That strengthened the sense of purpose and increased the membership and effectiveness of the organization.

Dual Supervisory System

We developed a dual supervisory system to use in the training of minority mental health professionals. Each trainee has an individual supervisor, usually from a different social background, and an ethnic consultant of the same race as the trainee. For the minority trainee working primarily with minority students, having an ethnic consultant who is a skilled clinician offers many obvious advantages. Among them are special clinical and cultural knowledge and the consultant's availability as a role model for the trainee.

The dual supervisory system can also be effective in dealing

47

with the main hazard of a minority-oriented training program: the tendency of trainees to overidentify with students whom they see professionally and to externalize their own learning problems, explaining them away on the basis of racism or the irrelevancy of what is being taught. The ethnic consultant is best able to confront distortions resulting from ethnocentricity through a process of reality testing based on an examination of the clinical material at hand.

Because experienced minority supervisors are in short supply, they serve as consultants, while a non-ethnic supervisor bears the primary teaching responsibility. The importance of that cannot be overemphasized if confusion is to be minimized for the trainees. The minority consultant does not evaluate, grade, or exclusively determine the educational regimen for the trainee. Instead he focuses on specific racial or ethnic factors in the treatment or learning situation. He is available to both the trainee and nonethnic supervisor to plan the education program.

Minority trainees often bring idiosyncratic problems to the learning situation. They predictably display a hypersensitivity to anything faintly resembling discrimination and prejudice. Responsive to the current cultural ethos, they often reject traditional clinical approaches as unsuitable and irrelevant for members of their own group. Eager to use their developing skills to help their own people, they may want to treat only patients from their own background, thereby avoiding the difficulty of learning to work effectively with people of other races. Without the help of a minority consultant, significant conflicts can develop between the trainee and the supervisor around those issues. The structure we have developed permits the trainee to turn to the ethnic consultant for his special knowledge as well as for help in reducing the resistance to learning.

The minority consultant can also be very helpful to the trainee and the supervisor at times of stress. For example, a minority trainee who was dissatisfied with his first evaluation threatened to appeal the matter to the administration of his university. The supervisor, who considered the evaluation objective and tactful, could not understand the trainee's angry reaction. In a detailed brief the trainee questioned the phrasing and sentence structure of the evaluation.

At this point the matter was referred to the ethnic consultant. He reviewed the evaluation with the trainee, searching for unwarranted or discriminatory statements. When none were found, the real issue surfaced: the trainee had enormously high expectations for himself and felt he knew more than the evaluation indicated. In this situation, the ethnic consultant was invaluable in clarifying the real issue and

48

in avoiding a confrontation as a defense against a painful but necessary acknowledgment.

The ethnic consultant is availble to act as a buffer when minority trainees accuse supervisors of racism. The main disadvantage for the trainee when racism becomes an issue is that it almost inevitably leads to unresolved tension between the trainee and supervisor. As a result, the supervisor is reluctant to teach and the trainee learns less.

In addition to the individual supervision of trainees there are three weekly conferences. The first focuses on the specific knowledge necessary for crisis treatment, including diagnostic considerations and psychotherapeutic techniques. Crisis situations encountered by trainees are considered in detail, alternating with didactic presentations on topics including psychopathology, use of psychiatric drugs, and neurological and physiological factors.

The second conference is an introduction to psychotherapy. It deals primarily with differential diagnosis, planning of appropriate treatment goals, and the unique clinical issues that emerge in long-term treatment as compared to crisis treatment. The third is a general meeting with an agenda that varies from week to week.

Outcome of the Program

With the establishment of the training program at City College, we hoped that the total experience would sharply increase the interest of all staff in working with residents of low-income and racial ghettos. That was accomplished. All six trainees who completed their training took paid positions where their primary responsibilities were providing services to the residents of racial and poverty ghettos. Two remained at City College, two work at similar student health services, and two are at inner-city community mental health centers. In addition, staff who had not yet completed their training and senior staff were so stimulated by their experiences that their commitment increased.

Subsequently, a trainee group essentially equivalent to the one described was selected for a second training year. Our experiences confirmed the value and uniqueness of the training program, which has now become a permanent part of the student health service at the college.

As a result of our experience during the first training year, a number of things have become clear. Trainees make a

49

special contribution at student health services because they are midway between students and established health professionals. The transitional status of the trainees gives them a perspective that is extremely helpful in developing both the training program and the services offered students. In their work outside the health service, they have informal contacts with large numbers of students. That enables the trainees to suggest improvements or new programs, to predict student reactions to new programs, to suggest ways of avoiding potential problems, and to marshall student support for new services. Many minority students establish a better working relationship with minority trainees than with more experienced Caucasian staff. That is particularly helpful when crisis treatment, which is of necessity brief, is the primary service offered.

Minority staff are also extremely important as role models for minority students, many of whom have had discouraging experiences with educational institutions, caretaking organizations, and facilities providing health services. The opportunity for students to meet informally on campus with health professionals who are from racial minorities is extremely important for students who are beginning to establish career goals. It is our impression that these personal encounters are far less frequent at more traditional field placements for graduate trainees.

We expected to encounter complex problems as the multiracial staff with widely varied backgrounds, professions, and experience developed ways to work effectively together. We were not disappointed. The staff varied from a 22-year-old first-year graduate student to senior staff who were working professionals before the youngest trainee was born. The generation gap waxed and waned as we dealt with conflictual issues. While the main feeling that developed was one of mutual respect and affection, there were both acute crises and continuing areas of disagreement.

It became clear, however, that the entire staff shared the same goal: to develop the best possible direct services and training experiences. It was not always clear how to do that. Ferment and stimulation inevitably developed from our planning, experimenting, and breaking new ground. Unity and determination grew as conflicts were met, grappled with, and resolved. Questions or complaints could be aired and resolved at regular meetings that everyone attended. They too helped unify the staff.

We believe we have demonstrated that planning and developing a training program for minority mental health professionals can

50

be a highly rewarding experience. It requires considering the special needs and interests of the trainees and arranging a specially designed program for them, but when that is done and the service works, the rewards far exceed the risks.

REFERENCES

Davis, K., and Swartz, J. Increasing Black Students' Utilization of Mental Health Services. American Journal of Orthopsychiatry, Vol. 42 (October, 1972), 771-776.

VI

CRISIS-ORIENTED PSYCHOTHERAPY: SOME THEORETICAL
AND PRACTICAL CONSIDERATIONS

Gerald Amada

Since its inception in January, 1970, over 3,000 different students have been provided abaout 8,000 hours of individual and group psychotherapy at the City College of San Francisco Mental Health Program. Although no arbitrary quota was placed on the number of therapeutic sessions to which students were entitled, each semester the average number of contacts per student was below three. City College students, particularly those in their late teens and early twenties, evidenced overriding concerns with respect to their emotional independence-dependence. Such concerns often resulted in a tendency to utilize therapeutic services on a relatively tentative and brief basis. The experience of organizing and implementing a communty college psychological service which primarily offers short-term psychotherapy stimulated theoretical interest in identifying those characteristics which distinguish crisis-oriented psychotherapy from other modalities of treatment.

A frequent question put to staff members of the Mental Health Program is, "Do you provide psychotherapy services or must students who require long-term assistance go elsewhere?" The presumptuous phrasing of the question, by implication, imputes to short-term psychotherapy a lesser status and importance than to long-range modalities of psychological intervention. Such a denigrating perspective actually does a serious disservice to the process, patient and psychotherapist involved in crisis-oriented therapeutic encounters.

What is a Crisis?

It is an emotionally significant event or radical change of

Reprinted with permission from the Journal of Contemporary Psychotherapy, Vol. 9, No. 1 (Spring-Summer, 1977).

status in a person's life which is disruptive of his usual mode of adaptation. Time-limited or crisis-oriented (fewer than nine sessions) psychotherapy is generally justified on two bases. First, funding and personnel shortages in many community psychiatric agencies require a form of psychotherapy designed to reach maximum populations. Thus, by structuring services toward the short-term resolution of psychological crises it is possible to effect adequate caseload turnover. By avoiding inordinately long treatment waiting periods an agency enhances its prospects for therapeutic success.

As indicated by Lewin, "the long wait for treatment insures that only the most regressed and dependent people remain, since those with any ego strengths have made arrangements for therapy elsewhere, a process of case selection which almost guarantees therapeutic failure" (Lewin, 1970).

A second valid basis for providing short-term psychotherapeutic services is the indisputable fact that the foremost concern of the vast majority of prospective psychiatric patients is immediate psychological relief and not basic personality transformation. It is manifestly illogical and self-defeating to gear a therapeutic philosophy and set of clinical techniques primarily to the luxuries of long-term contact when the preponderance of psychiatric patients are more amenable to short-term modalities. The fact that short-term psychotherapy is ubiquitously the mainstay of public and private psychiatric services makes it imperative to examine and delineate those clinical characteristics which are peculiar to short-term intervention.

It is ordinarily sensible and therapeutic to regard any cause or reason a psychiatric patient employs for seeking psychotherapy as a legitimate expression of a personal crisis which requires prompt psychotherapeutic help. There are exceptional instances when psychotherapy is unwarranted and contraindicated due to external coercive demands upon the patient; however, such circumstances are relatively rare and a subject for another discussion. Although the verbalized emotional concerns of the patient who enters psychotherapy may not constitute the "actual" crisis, there are few therapeutic pitfalls to genuinely regarding the patient as someone who is indeed in a state of crisis. A psychotherapist who, regardless of theoretical orientation, approaches all new patients as persons in crisis will be in a position of readiness to help overcome the patient's and his own tendency to emotionally trivialize important but sometimes subtle psychodynamic factors.

To regard all initial contacts as crisis-engendered does not

54

in the least imply an alarmist or pessimistic viewpoint. On the contrary, such a perspective implies a hopeful conviction that a genuine resolution of the precipitating crisis will restore even the most seriously disturbed patient to a level of psychological functioning which the latter regards as adaptive and viable. Therefore, to aspire with the patient toward crisis-resolution is frequently in total accordance with both the ostensible and unexpressed wishes of the patient.

A common criticism of crisis-oriented psychotherapy is that it tends to neglect or minimize the importance of long-standing, basic personality conflicts. This is untrue both on practical and theoretical grounds. The short-term psychotherapist carefully evaluates and incorporates characterologic factors in formulating a diagnosis and in implementing the treatment plan. He may detect repetitive patterns and themes which stem from early childhood that require explication and dynamic interpretation. Although time limitations may preclude the emergence and fruitful interpretation of many deep-seated and steadfastly resisted emotional conflicts, basic personality factors are not left untouched in brief clinical encounters. As a matter of fact, effective crisis-intervention will not only reduce psychological pain but will frequently produce important insights into the personality which enable the patient to forcefully discover how and why he falls prone to crises. Such discoveries can have the highly salutary effect of fortifying the patient against future psychological mishaps and, thus, serve as inestimable sources of self-esteem which enhance the potentialities of personality. The following case exemplifies this point.

A female student, age 21, in an initial session described feelings of depression which, although long-standing, became particularly acute during the time of a family reunion from which she voluntarily excluded herself. Her reason for estranging herself from her family was to avoid contact with her father whom she had not seen in over seven years. During this session the patient revealed that at age 14 her father had expressed a desire to have regular sexual relations with her, for which she would be financially remunerated. Shocked, dismayed and humiliated, she immediately decamped, vowing never to see him again; a pledge she faithfully kept. However, the patient grew more depressed each subsequent year and found herself increasingly desirous of a reconciliation.

In discussing her current feelings toward her father, the patient admitted both rage and an attitude of forgiveness. She revealed that her primary apprehension in seeing her father again was that he would again "proposition" her. In response to

concerns raised by the patient, the therapist set out to assist
her with four interconnected questions: (1) What was the status
of her father's mental condition when she was 14?, (2) Would she
benefit psychologically from a substantive reconciliation with
him?, (3) How should she respond in the event that he were to
attempt a sexual overture?, and (4) Should she remind her father
of the incident which originally estranged them in order to mend
old wounds?

Brief exploration revealed that the patient's father
underwent multiple psychiatric hospitalizations during her
adolescence. In discussing the nature of those hospitalizations
it became clear that his behavior seven years before was a
psychotic manifestation. Gradually she began to view him in a
more objective and less condemnatory light. From this
recognition flowed the determination to see her father again.
She independently resolved that all sexual overtures would be
dealt with firmly and emphatically. Because she herself could
not decide whether to remind her father of the earlier debacle,
she was encouraged by the therapist to totally avoid mention of
the incident if possible. The patient then scheduled a second
session for a week hence.

The patient reported the following week that she had
enjoyed a remarkably unproblematic visit with her father. He was
kind and considerate, albeit occasionally disoriented. In
parting, they planned to see each other often. The patient
expressed the exhilarated feeling that a mountain had been lifted
from her shoulders and that her staggering depression had
vanished. No future therapeutic contacts were scheduled and none
eventuated. A year later the therapist and student met
accidentally on campus, affording the former the opportunity to
learn that she and her father had further solidified their
relationship and that she continued to be free of debilitating
depressions. School performance, social relationships and
vocational effectiveness were also mentioned as areas in which
marked improvement took place. She made unsolicited reference to
the transformative value of the psychotherapy.

The following discussion deals with the therapeutic
philosophy and techniques which are inherent in brief
psychotherapy. The considerations referred to here are not
exhaustive and are not exclusively applicable to short-term
treatment. The intent here is merely to adumbrate the
distinguising features and thrusts of short-term psychotherapy
and not to place unnecessary restraints upon the options
available in long-term work.

Attention to Time-Limitations

Particularly in psychiatric agencies which give statistical evidence of a preponderance of short-term cases, the psychotherapist is well disposed to regard the initial interview as potentially his last session with the patient. Such a therapeutic stance should not be cause for impotent anxiety, premature interventions or professional pessimism. Rather, it is a realistic recognition of the fact that the psychotherapist must actively mobilize his clinical skills in a manner commensurate with the unique potentials and demands of a markedly time-limited contact. A psychotherapist who is sensitively attuned and reponsive to the possibility of early termination will enhance his chances for therapeutic success. Furthermore, his heightened attention to time (perhaps in the form of highly pointed questioning, lively and supportive interpretative responses and a willing opinionatedness) not only will promote therapeutic impact but will also improve the prospects that the patient will return for additional services if warranted. Ironically, many patients fail to return for much needed subsequent psychotherapeutic sessions precisely because the psychotherapist casually and mistakenly assumed he would have ample future contact with the patient.

Establishing a Chronology

One of the first tasks of crisis-intervention is to establish a chronology or sequence of important psychological events. The psychotherapist presumes that a significant interpersonal or intrapsychic event has "broken the camel's back" in precipitating the crisis. Although he should not be overly stringent in delimiting the patient's discussion of overall concerns, he must determinedly strive to gain a coherent, sequential picture of the precipitants of the crisis. By thoughtfully tracing the events which have undermined the patient's emotional life the patient gains a functional awareness of what psychological and pragmatic steps are necesssary in order to reverse the destructive process and restore his equilibrium.

Utilization of Ancillary Services

A patient in acute psychological crisis often has a variety of needs which can be met only through the provision of a variety of ancillary services. Examples of such services are the legal, welfare, medical, dental, vocational and educational resources of the community. Commonly, in long-term psychotherapy there are contraindications to directly assisting the patient in gaining access to community agencies. Such intervention can unduly contaminate the long-term therapuetic relationship or foster an

57

an inordinate dependency upon the therapist which is inimical to the patient's growth.

In short-term therapy, however, certain types of crises may not be amenable to an approach which is exclusively psychological, in the narrow sense of the term. For example, a patient who is about to be evicted from his apartment may suffer acute separation anxieties which require psychological intervention. It may serve his interest to also receive timely legal, housing and economic assistance. The crisis interventionist who is conversant with those agencies of the community which provide such services is in an advantageous position to help the patient with a referral, particularly if the latter lacks the knowledge or sophistication to initiate the enlistment of community agencies himself. The minimal risk of relationship contamination and the fostering of excessive dependency in short-term psychotherapy is taken in order to reap the more immediate benefit of crisis-resolution.

Heightened Therapeutic Activity

Determined structuring of a crisis-oriented interview is based upon the willingness and ability of the psychotherapist to be relatively active. An active psychotherapist is not necessarily disputatious, rude, or inhibitory. On the contrary, persons in crisis tend to justifiably regard the psychotherapist's non-intrusively active manner as an indication of interest, involvement and encouragement. It has been observed that certain passive forms of therapeutic intervention, such as protracted listening and wooden neutrality, give rise to a patient's expectations that he can and should delay resolution of his crisis, sometimes resulting in unduly lengthy and frustrating therapeutic work. Conversely, an active psychotherapist in a time-limited clinical situation will convey implicitly and explicitly a realistic expectation that an early resolution of the presenting crisis is achievable. Often it is exactly that expectation which serves as the primary therapeutic agent.

Maintenance of a Positive Relationship

A time-limited therapeutic encounter requires that the therapist seek to maintain a positive relationship with the patient. Such a posture does not preclude exploration of aggressive, hostile attitudes which are necessarily engendered by the therapeutic milieu. However, by permissively allowing or fostering intense and prolonged negative feelings toward the therapist in abbreviated therapeutic work, the psychotherapist defeats his own credibility as a source of psychological benefit.

In crisis-oriented work it is incumbent upon the psychotherapist to quickly gain the patient´s trust and confidence in his competence. The patient´s relatively positive feelings for the psychotherapist´s personality and clinical skills will be, in large part, the principal springboard to restoring homeostasis.

Use of the Contemporary Context

In long-term psychotherapy it is often appropriate and desirable to encourage temporary regression through the patient´s recollections of childhood experiences. The psychotherapist, by relevantly comparing and applying contemporaneous events to the patient´s recent and distant past, helps him regress to an irrational thought process which permits the formulation of a new conception or an especially clear delineation of a problem.

Even a single therapeutic session can generate extensive historical material and intense irrational thought processes. As suggested above, such regression can serve to enhance the self-awareness and growth of the ego. However, in brief psychotherapy, time-limitations may leave the patient highly vulnerable to the ambiguity of his regressive thought processes. Rather than utilizing the regression toward realistic ends, he may become victimized, for lack of therapeutic time, by an inability to adequately return to rational thinking. Therefore, in brief psychotherapy, it is necessary to make a conscientious effort to place historical data and irrational associations in a proper contemporary context. This is not to suggest that brief therapy discourages or ignores regressive activity, but only that the patient´s regressive thoughts be readily applied to his current dilemma in order that he can begin effectively broaching the immediate task of crisis-resolution.

The Role of Apparel, Vernacular and Office Furnishings

The appearance, speech and office furnishings of the psychotherapist are frequent catalysts of significant, symbolic responses in the patient. Long-term psychotherapy tends to afford abundant opportunity to address and explore those responses. However, when in short-term psychotherapy the office appearance, speech and apparel of the psychotherapist inadvertently alienate the patient, there may be too little time to profitably elicit and resolve the latter´s antagonism. The author is not recommending that the short-term psychotherapist dress, speak and furnish his office in total conformity with the norms of his patients, whatever they might be. However, in dealing with patients primarily on a short-term basis, it is particularly important to be unflaggingly cognizant of the role of these factors and to consider possible alternatives of

personal apparel, speech, and office appearance which do not
offend or alienate.

Relinquishment of Anonymity

In brief psychotherapeutic encounters which have an
arbitrarily appointed termination date, the psychotherapist
should be prepared to relinquish a degree of his professional
opaqueness and anonymity. Obviously, there are definite
therapeutic risks in sharing personal information with the
patient. Nevertheless, the psychotherapist who provides brief
services may be more therapeutically effective if he can
discreetly and selectively shed some of his persona. Often
therapeutic failure results from an unnecessarily uncharitable
coyness and retentiveness on the part of the short-term
psychotherapist. Given the fact that certain personal
information about the psychotherapist cannot prudently be
imparted and that all such personal data is potentially
contaminating and subject to misusage, a too rigid adherence to
total anonymity may severely alienate the patient, subvert the
patient-therapist alliance and thereby neutralize all therapeutic
advancements.

Flexible Scheduling

Brief psychotherapy in particular requires a responsive
flexibility of scheduling. Unlike the predictable regularity of
scheduled sessions which is common to conventional long-term
psychotherapy, crisis-oriented services must be geared to a wide
variety of scheduling options. The expected range may reasonably
be from multiple sessions within the same day to an arrangement
by which the psychotherapist is placed on an availability basis
in order to trouble-shoot crises whenever and however they arise.
In addition, the length of sessions may vary in accordance with
the patient´s emotional needs and tolerance. A psychotherapist
who "stands on ceremony" by insisting that all patients utilize
his services only at regular, convenient intervals will
inevitably and necessarily exclude large numbers of treatable
patients from his practice.

Telephone Accessibility

Brief psychotherapeutic intervention in particular
frequently requires a special willingness on the part of the
psychotherapist to be reached by telephone. As indicated by
Mackinnon and Michels (1971), the telephone plays an important
role in contemporary psychiatric practice. Although patients in
crisis may not actually avail themselves of telephone access to
the psychotherapist, the fact that they are encouraged to contact

60

him in the event of an emergency, often allays anxiety and works toward resolving the crisis. Dealing with psychological crises in a time-limited modality especially requires an explicitly reassuring, protective and nurturing professional attitude. Offering himself generously for emergency telephone contacts effectively betokens and conveys such a therapeutic attitude to the patient. The therapeutic impact of this attitude has been particularly evident to this author when he himself has taken the initiative to contact his crisis-ridden patients by telephone.

The Provision of Intellectual "Handles"

The provision of intellectual "anchors" or "handles" is an especially useful therapeutic tool in brief psychotherapy. Many confusional states make it impossible for the patient to define or clarify his feelings. At times words will be misapplied to feelings such as a reference to "annoyance" when the patient actually feels rage. Commonly the misdesignation of words to feelings will further exacerbate disruptive emotions. The patient feels a nebulous, indefinable, unnameable fear for which he cannot account. He then finds it impossible to master or manage feelings which he cannot rationally circumscribe. The following example is relevant: a student patient at the College Health Center returned for a second session in a much improved psychological condition. When asked by the psychotherapist what he thought were the reasons for his gains, he remarked glowingly that he discovered why he was upset. He stated, "It's because I'm anxious." Puzzled, the psychotherapist probed for deeper, more complicated explanations, tending to debunk the student's contribution to the matter. After considerable fruitless investigation, it became clear that the student was basically correct. He had constructively applied to himself a term (anxiety) used by the psychotherapist in the first session. The word was pregnant with important meaning to the student and helped to demystify his fears and inhibitions. The crisis interventionist must recognize the overwhelmingly destructive effect of bewilderment upon the patient and conscientiously seek to supply him with the ballast of a definitive working vocabulary with which he can explain and govern his own feelings.

The Provision of Advice

The role of advice-giving as a psychotherapeutic technique is controversial. This author recognizes a high degree of validity to Ocsar Wilde's witty aphorism that, "to give advice is foolish. To give good advice is fatal." Nevertheless, there are certain junctures in crisis-oriented psychotherapy when advice-giving is essential. For example, a patient who possesses a weapon with which he plans mayhem may require directives to relinquish the weapon and submit to hospitalization. A patient with a too severe superego who is unwittingly suffering through repeated academic misfortunes may benefit from advice to disenroll. A patient who has prematurely and unwisely terminated psychotherapy elsewhere may need overt encouragement to return to his former therapist. Traditional psychotherapists have been rather allergic to supplying advice to their patients on the grounds that it is inefficaceous and fosters unhealthy dependence. In short-term psychotherapy the hazard of fostering undesirable dependency is recognized and carefully weighed against the potential benefits of crisis-resolution through corrective decision-making. Especially in crisis-intervention work it is important to appreciate the fact that certain psychiatric patients cannot disencumber themselves of severely impoverishing entanglements without being authoritatively advised to do so. Although time-limitations will probably not allow for the development of intense dependency conflicts such as frequently evolve in long-term treatment, it is usually best that advice be accorded sparingly, gingerly, and optionally in order that the patient feel free to go his own way.

A Special Repertoire

Finally, short-term psychotherapy requires a special repertoire of clinical styles and interventions which are professionally and personally exacting. It may necessitate unorthodox therapeutic interventions such allowing friends, instructors and other significant persons to directly participate in the therapeutic process. It may require that the psychotherapist meet with the patient in an extramural setting such as a classroom, school. cafeteria or the patient´s own home (Amada and Swartz, 1972). In certain crisis-serving psychiatric facilities the practitioner must expect to encounter patients with whom he will have to intervene physically in order to prevent personal harm to the patient or himself. In certain instances he might gain considerable therapeutic mileage by offering patients cigarettes or refreshments.

This is not to imply that the author advocates that the psychotherapist become a dilettante or prestidigitator who deftly plies a therapeutic bag of tricks to charm and placate his crisis-ridden patients. Although special clinical circumstances sometimes warrant unorthodox interventions, the clinician must exercise particular discretion and care when he departs from conventional therapeutic procedures.

Although the goals of long-term and crisis-oriented psychotherapy may, in some therapeutic situations, coincide or overlap, the two modalities mandate disparate therapeutic approaches. In sum, the standard of clinical adeptness and sophistication requisite for undertaking effective short-term psychotherapy is unique, and perhaps even more difficult to achieve than that which inheres in long-term psychotherapy.

REFERENCES

Amada, Gerald and Swartz, J. Social Work in a College Mental Health Program. Journal of Social Casework, Vol. 53 (1972), 528-533.

Lewin, Karl K. Brief Encounters. St.Louis: Warren H. Green, Inc., 1970.

Mackinnon, Roger A., and Michels, Robert. Psychiatric Interview in Clinical Practice. Philadelphia: W.B. Saunders, 1971.

VII

THE INTERLUDE BETWEEN SHORT- AND

LONG-TERM PSYCHOTHERAPY

Gerald Amada

The interlude between short- and long-term psychotherapy is ordinarily characterized by the following developments: (1) an increasing vagueness with respect to formerly circumscribed psychological goals, (2) the assumption on the part of the therapist of a less active role in the treatment process, and (3) the emerging centrality of the transference relationship to the therapeutic process.

The resolution of crisis in the early phases of psychotherapeutic treatment may give rise to certain new and sometimes unwieldy dilemmas that require the vigilant attention and understanding of the clinician. As the regressive impact of the crisis diminishes and the patient develops better ego functioning, he may spontaneously experience a significant loss of his former intense commitment to the therapeutic process and to the therapist himself.

Termination or Prolongation

As the patient improves, the therapist must determine the following: (1) The extent to which the patient has substantively overcome, and perhaps even psychologically matured from, his personal crisis. For example, is the patient seemingly manifesting self-control, light-heartedness, and adequacy as a defense against conflicted feelings toward the therapist (i.e., "flight into health," or "transference cure"? 1 Or, conversely, has the patient undergone a genuine and salutary resolution of his crisis, thus requiring no further psychotherapeutic

Reprinted with permission from the American Journal of Psychotherapy, Vol. XXXVII, No. 3 (July, 1983).

intervention? (2) Does the psychotherapist recommend or at least support the discontinuance of psychotherapy or should he favor its extension for the purpose of further exploring pathological and/or problematic personality issues?

Whether the therapist recommends termination or prolongation of therapy will likely depend upon his assessment of the degree to which the patient has genuinely resolved his crisis. If, in the therapist's opinion, the patient has achieved reasonable resolution of his crisis and, furthermore, the patient evidences minimal interest in undertaking ongoing psychotherapy, the therapist's options are narrower and more obvious. In this event, in all likelihood, the decision to discontinue treatment will be reached as a mutual and incontestably satisfactory course of action. According to MacLean et al., a patient's explicit knowledge of the planned discontinuance of time-limited therapy may even serve as a possible spur to his psychological improvement.2

However, when the therapist and the patient jointly recognize the necessity or potential benefits of prolonging their relationship, there are certain theoretical and practical considerations which, quite naturally, assume clinical importance. This paper will attempt to present those considerations that the author regards as particularly relevant in dealing with the transitional phase between short- and long-term psychotherapy.

The Increased Ambiguity of Therapeutic Purposes and Goals

The patient who initially enters psychotherapy ordinarily harbors rather explicit and circumscribed psychological objectives to which he aspires, albeit, often with great difficulty. These objectives may, for example, include relief from depression and anxiety, freedom from a problematic personal relationship, or the improved self-control of intense, eruptive emotions.

Although the patient may manifest a degree of concern with the inner workings of his own personality (workings that perhaps played a significant role in precipitating the crisis in the first place), these concerns often assume secondary importance to the patient seeking immediate resolution of psychological stress.3 Therefore, unless basic personality issues are introduced into the psychotherapeutic process prior to or at the point of the patient's resolution of crisis, the resolution itself may leave the patient with a dread that a dangerous void awaits him in the therapy. At this therapeutic juncture the patient might validly inquire of the therapist, "Well, now that

66

I've gotten over that tough hurdle, where do we go from here?"

How the psychotherapist responds to this query will depend upon several factors: (1) The extent to which the therapist has already piqued and enlisted the patient's interest in his own personality in the earlier phases of the therapy, (2) the level of motivation, sophistication, and insight that the patient manifests regarding his own personality, and (3) the patient's amenability to the furtherance of psychotherapeutic work.

The therapist who is queried with, "What do we cover now?," should not automatically assume that all such probings are manifestations of an infantile wish to be gratified or controlled. Nor should he too perfunctorily interpret such a question to be the characteristic feigned ignorance of the passive-aggressive personality. The psychotherapist must carefully consider such possibilities before responding to his patients. In the event that he perceives the patient's probings for clarification as an unrealistic quest for reassurance, it may indeed be wise to call attention to and analyze the unconscious motives and defenses that underlie the patient's behavior.

Other, perhaps more salient considerations may arise at this juncture in the therapeutic process. The therapist, especially during the transitional phase of therapy, might validly consider the following question: To what extent can a patient who is relatively uninitiated to therapy realistically understand and foresee such an extraordinarily complex experience, an experience that the therapist himself has grasped and mastered only after many years of disciplined training? Logic and common sense require that the therapist take into account the fact that the patient who has never undergone long-term treatment will find many aspects of continuing therapy to be unintelligible and bewildering.

As Reik has suggested, a considerable degree of the challenge and psychological benefit to be derived from psychotherapy is provided by the unexpected vicissitudes and surprises that invariable emerge during the course of treatment.[4] Furthermore, many psychotherapists who have extensive experience in providing long-term treatment will readily admit that a good number of the turns, setbacks, advances, and outcomes that take place during therapy are entirely unpredictable and sometimes quite uncanny. Is the psychotherapist, for these reasons, to remain totally noncommital in his posture towards the patient seeking clarification regarding the future workings and results of long-term treatment? I think not. The following are some of the therapeutic intereventions that I have found particularly useful and beneficial to patients who are considering long-term

67

treatment after a course of brief psychotherapy.

Realistic Optimism

One of the foremost and obvious concerns of the patient is
whether he will "get better." Such a wish may encompass hopes
for symptomatic relief, improved insight and understanding,
greater sociality, enhancement of creative expression, etc.
Whether the patient´s hopes of "getting better" are realistic or
magical, he is entitled, especially during the transitional phase
of therapy, to receive some indication from his therapist
regarding the latter´s capacity and desire to help him. Naturally
the therapist should neither convey categorical promises,
predictions, and guarantees to the patient, since such an
approach is inherently fraught with painful disappointment and
disillusionment; nor express, implicitly or explicitly, a
woodenly neutral or pessimistic outlook to the patient lest he,
thereby, erect a formidable barrier to therapeutic success. The
therapists´s poor morale and indifferent outlook will unavoidably
instill in his patient similar attitudes and, consequently, will
be deterrents to the treatment. In such a circumstance the
therapist would probably do well to refer the patient to another
clinician.

If, and only if, the therapist genuinely and realistically
believes that he can help his patient, then there are few
hazards, particularly during the transitional phase of therapy,
attached to his imparting such a conviction to the patient. This
vital conviction should be transmitted without reference to rigid
timetables for psychological change. The mere fact that the
therapist truly believes and is willing to impart that he can
help the patient "become better" will very possibly establish
itself as the most fundamental underpinning of the therapeutic
process itself. Naturally, the incredulous patient will attempt
to rebut and perhaps even subvert the therapist´s optimistic
convictions. If so, the therapist will need to deal with these
suspicious and negativistic reactions by helping the patient
explore their diverse origins, and thereby, consider the
possiblity of developing an allliance with the therapist.5
Again, the hope and optimism of the therapist, when genuine and
convincing, is essential to assisting the patient who is passing,
with deep feelings of doubt and futility, through the
transitional phase of therapy.

Explanations Regarding the Shift from Relative
Activity to Relative Inactivity

The psychotherapist engaged in crisis-oriented
psycotherapeutic work ordinarily tends to be relatively active in

68

his stance towards the patient. As the patient resolves and overcomes his initial crisis he commonly will require less zestful activity on the part of the therapist. He will perhaps begin to realize that largely through expressing and exploring his concerns in therapy he can acquire greater self-esteem and interpersonal satisfaction. Consequently, the therapist may concomitantly and deliberately prepare himself for gradually assuming a more retiring and unstructured role. It is at this watershed period in the treatment that a particular clinical intervention may be warranted.

Is the therapist to assume that the patient possesses sufficient understanding of the therapeutic process to realize the rationales and bases for the therapist´s growing withdrawal from him? Hardly. It is conceivable that the psychologically sophisticated patient will correctly interpret the therapist´s reasons for his planned withdrawal. It is equally likely that the patient confronted with the therapist´s unexplained withdrawal will come to his own, perhaps quite unfounded, conclusions regarding the basis for this shift in their relationship. For example, he may erroneously conclude that the therapist has been developing a dislike for him or that he has offended and disturbed the therapist with his emotional problems. He may, therefore, perceive the therapist´s altering role as retaliatory and punitive; as harsh punishment for some vague impropriety or personality trait that the therapist cannot brook. If he possesses an adequate degree of confidence, the patient may query the therapist about the unexpected shift between them and thus demystify the phenomenon. If he does not possess such confidence, he may frantically and prematurely terminate his treatment.

What is required of the therapist when he discerns that the patient is dealing with this crossroads in the treatment with undue trepidation and suspicion? As in the case of the patient´s afore-mentioned doubts regarding his capacity to "get better," the therapist might explore and interpret the various origins and transference significance of the patient´s distorted imaginings about their perceptibly altered relationship.

However, the patient who reaches such an impasse in the therapy may require a rather clear explanation from the therapist relative to the rationales, goals, and implications of the therapist´s increasingly passive interactive posture. An explanation of the goals and purposes of the therapist´s modified stance may serve to enhance the patient´s awareness of the therapeutic process itself, further promote the growth of a positive transference and ultimately enlist the patient´s ego in effectively resolving his concerns. In any case, it is probably

a mistake to automatically assume that the patient clearly
discerns the therapist's actual reasons for reducing his activity
level. Although the therapist should be alive to the patient's
imaginings and suspicions regarding his modified stance, acute
anxiety reactions may often be precluded by simple statements
regarding the rationales for the change.

Explanations Regarding the Growing Centrality of Transference-related Issues

As the patient and therapist continue to regularly interact,
over a period of time their relationship spontaneously
intensifies and eventually assumes a quite central position, both
within and without the therapy itself, in the emotional life of
the patient.6 As the therapeutic relationship heightens in
emotional importance, the patient quite naturally develops more
highly charged attitudes and feelings towards the therapist, only
some of which may be conscious and self-explanatory. Because
these attitudes increasingly occupy central importance in the
patient's emotional life they come to possess the potential for
either undermining or furthering therapeutic objectives.

As the patient's feelings and attitudes towards the
therapist intensify, the therapist must commensurately assume the
onus for eliciting and interpreting them. To avoid this task
will often invite one of two results: (1) The patient will soon
become overwhelmed by inexplicable and, therefore, unmanageable
emotions and, rather than broach this matter with the therapist,
will bolt, i.e., will prematurely terminate his treatment, or (2)
the patient will deal with his mysterious and uncontrollable
feelings towards the therapist by withholding them from the
therapist and acting them out in other "safer" relationships.
This tendency can result in quite compulsive and self-defeating
behavior and, as a result, serves to "prove" to the patient that
therapy only tends to aggravate his problems. In this manner,
premature termination may be decided upon by the patient as his
only logical and viable course of action.

During the interlude between short- and long-term treatment
the therapist must exercise particular discretion in how he
elicits and interprets the patient's attitudes towards him. A
therapist who too matter-of-factly and unexpectedly attempts to
plumb such feelings may not sufficiently appreciate the degree of
dread that many patients harbor over expressing these emotions.
Many patients have never spoken openly and directly of their
"true" feelings towards others. Consequently, even the gentlest
invitation by a therapist for a patient to reflect upon and
verbalize feelings towards him may arouse exaggerated suspicions,
concerns, and apprehensions. For example, the patient may

70

misperceive the therapist´s probings as indications of the therapist´s displeasure or impatience with him, i.e., that the therapist is personally upset with the manner in which the patient is treating him. Or, an unduly insecure and suspicious patient may be inclined to regard the therapist´s interest in his emotional reactions to their relationship as an artifice, used to gain the patient´s trust or affection as leverage for later retaliation.

How, then, does the therapist deal with the dilemma of igniting interest in and discussion of the therapeutic relationship and, at the same time, responding to the patient´s inner turmoil over expressing his thoughts on such a highly charged issue?

<u>Case Example</u>

A forty-five-year old woman entered therapy for the first time while suffering from severe depression. In her marriage she was harried and denigrated by her husband. When she objected to this mistreatment, he ridiculed her objections and called her "crazy." This sometimes caused her to doubt her sanity. Eventually she ceased objecting and suppressed her rage. In discussing her childhood, the patient described her father as tyrannical and terrifying. He would repeatedly ridicule the patient, drive her to despair and tears and then accuse her of being a self-pitying "sourpuss."

After several sessions the patient evidenced an increase in anxiety and wariness towards the therapist. Her speech became studied and she tended to prevent the therapist from completing his comments. Since this tendency persisted and intensified, the therapist called attention to it by asking whether something troubled the patient about their sessions. The patient immediately became more anxious and leery, demanding to know why the therapist was bringing up the matter.

The therapist shared his observation that the patient seemed increasingly anxious during their sessions and wondered whether she might have concerns about him that were associated with the inhumane treatment she had received from her husband and her father. The patient hurriedly acknowledged that the very same thought had occurred to her, but quite suddenly fell into a state of panic and with great vehemence demanded to know why the therapist was calling attention to how she felt about him. (It seemed that the patient´s troubled relationships with her husband and her father caused her to view the therapist´s inquiry as a harsh criticism calculated to demean and humiliate her.)

71

The therapist realized that further interpretations of the patient's suspicions about his intentions would only aggravate rather than neutralize them. It was clear that the patient's fears could be defused only by an explanation of the therapist's behavior.

At this point the therapist told the patient that he had several reasons for inquiring into her feelings about him. First, if these feelings were troublesome to her, they would tend to inhibit her freedom of expression during the sessions and, consequently, would reduce the benefit to be derived from therapy. Second, by more fully understanding the nature of her relationship to the therapist. the patient would very likely gain insights into the other important emotional relationships in her life. Finally, by resolving many of the fears amd inhibitions she felt towards the therapist, the patient would probably experience less insecurity and dread generally. In short, the therapist's comments were formulated with the following purpose in mind: (1) To provide the patient with an understanding of the therapeutic relationship as a microcosm of her earlier, significant emotional relationships and (2) to assist the patient to realize that the therapeutic relationship, if adequately understood, could be a valuable springboard for psychological growth.

The patient considered the therapist's remarks for several minutes and then conceded that, although she did not fully understand "how all this works," it seemed to make sense. Her fears greatly subsided. Although there were many times throughout the remaining course of therapy when the patient became highly suspicious and enraged by the therapist's references to the therapeutic relationship, she often found the therapist's above-mentioned explanation to be a reliable basis for reexploring her feelings about him.

The intervention described in the case example had several weighty advantages. It appealed to the patient's "observing ego" and, therefore, served to neutralize her most adverse reactions.7 It also reflected the therapist's willingness to share with the patient some of the underlying dynamics of the methods he intended to use to help her, thus, providing some impetus to the patient for sharing the inner dynamics of her own thoughts and concerns. Perhaps most importantly, such an intervention may be legitimately perceived by the patient as an earnest gesture or "gift," offered by the therapist to promote and cement what is basically a genuinely human relationship. For this reason, such an intervention, when used properly, can have considerable value in fostering the therapeutic alliance. That alliance will undoubtedly become a central element in enabling patient and

72

therapist to surmount and resolve the special dilemmas which they will face during the interlude phase of therapy.

Summary

The interlude between short- and long-term psychotherapy is a critical period, fraught with possible pitfalls as well as therapeutic opportunities. During this transitional phase certain discernible shifts may take place in the therapeutic process. Among these changes are: (1) an increasing vagueness with respect to formerly circumscribed goals and outcomes, (2) the assumption on the part of the therapist of a less active role in the treatment process, and (3) the growing centrality and significance of the transference relationship to the therapeutic process.

Each of these shifts will very likely evoke strong and sometimes frightening reactions in the patient. These reactions can often be effectively broached and resolved through discussion and interpretation of their earlier origins. An effective auxiliary approach, however, is the willingness of the therapist to impart to the confused or frightened patient his rationales for being less definitive regarding therapeutic goals, less active in pursuing those goals, and more explicitly interested in the patient´s attitudes towards him.

REFERENCES

1. Firestein, Stephen K. Termination in Psychoanalysis. International Universities Press, New York, 1978.

2. Maclean, G., MacIntosh, B.-A.,Taylor, A., and Gerber, M. A Clinical Approach to Brief Dynamic Psychotherapies in Child Pscyhiatry. Can. J. Psychiatry, 27:113, 1982.

3. Amada, Gerald. Crisis-Oriented Psychotherapy: Some Theoretical and Practical Considerations. J. Contemp. Psychother., 9:104, 1977.

4. Reik, Theodore. Surprise and the Psychoanalyst. Paul, French, Trubner, London, 1936.

5. Greenson, Ralph. The Technique and Practice of Psychoanalysis. International Universities Press, New York, 1967.

6. Amada, G. A Guide to Psychotherapy. University Press of America, Washington, D.C., 1983.

73

REFERENCES (CONT.)

7. Wallerstein, Robert   S.   Psychotherapy and Psychoanalysis.
   International Universities Press, New York, 1975.

74

VIII

SOCIAL WORK IN A COLLEGE MENTAL HEALTH PROGRAM

Gerald Amada, Jacqueline Swartz

Social workers are rarely found in a college setting, even though the diversity of their training and knowledge of community resources would seem to make them singularly appropriate as helping professionals for college students. At City College of San Francisco, social workers worked productively in a variety of ways within the context of the Mental Health Program. This article describes the ways in which social workers were utilized in the Mental Health Program. It is hoped that such utilization, although unique at this time, will serve as an encouraging model for use in the future.

Short-term Therapy

The Mental Health Program is geared toward providing short-term crisis therapy mainly on an individual basis. Because the majority of students are in their late teens or early twenties, there were certain problems or themes which emerged with marked regularity. Critical career choices, difficult relations with parents, complex marital choices and decisions, economic pressures, academic stresses, conflicts in relation to drugs and sex, and identity crises were found to constitute problems common to this age group. After a small number of sessions -- usually two to five -- students very often reached a satisfactory resolution or mitigation of their crises and required no further treatment. Students whose problems did require long-term therapy were referred to agencies in the San Francisco area.

From January 1970 through June 1971, 2,000 individual

Reprinted from Social Casework, November, 1972, by permission of the publishers, Family Service Association of America.

treatment hours were provided to a total of 600 students by four psychiatric social workers, three psychiatrists, and eight trainees from several disciplines. There were a significant number of students who presented emotional disturbances of a severe nature. In some instances it was necessary to see these students two or more times a week in order to provide sufficiently intensive treatment. Many of the students who came for treatment revealed overwhelming reality problems, such as lack of money for food, the necessity to work long hours in addition to studying and attending classes, and living conditions so crowded that studying was impossible. Attention was given to social and economic factors or agents of disturbance, and, accordingly, intrapsychic disorders were placed in perspective. Thus the clinical work was done in the context of social problems.

Glenn is a 25-year-old, married, second-year student who was referred to the Student Health Services by the dean of men. For about one year he had been seriously abusing himself with amphetamines which resulted in physical enervation, a marked deterioration in his academic performance, and a tenuous marital situation. Glenn had already been admitted to a state university for his junior year, contingent upon successful completion of his current courses. However, due to extreme fear and confusion, Glenn disenrolled from several of his courses prematurely and thereby jeopardized his chances to attend the university. It was only several days later that he recognized the gravity of his action.

Since there were only two months remaining in the semester, the therapist immediately offered regular and frequent sessions to Glenn. Initially, Glenn was advised about the various ways in which he could gain reenrollment in his courses. He approached the appropriate college administrators, who granted his request to reenroll. Throughout the first several sessions, therapy was directed toward supporting Glenn's efforts to reduce his drug intake. Although he could not sustain total drug abstinence, he was able to gradually reduce drug usage to a more tolerable level, enabling him to cope more competently with his course work.

After several sessions, emphasis was placed upon his marital relationship. In the last stages of this brief therapy, Glenn was encouraged to attend more actively to the early origins of his psychological problems. This investigation revealed important repetitive patterns of self-destructive behavior, many of which were clearly derived from early conflicts within the family matrix.

Another important context for therapy was the campus setting which varied according to where the crisis occurred. Therapists found themselves called to classrooms, offices, campus grounds, the cafeteria, and the library. In addition to seeing students in these various locations, it was often necessary to respond with the instructor or administrator present. An additional feature of the college setting involved extramural contact with students in therapy. Staff had to be prepared for accidental contact and could not rely on maintaining the anonymity possible in a clinic. For example, it was likely that a therapist might meet in the library a student who had discussed problems he would not want to reveal outside the privacy of the office. Sensitive issues arose that had to be dealt with in an extramural contact in which it was important to maintain confidentiality as well as the continuity of the relationship. Therapists learned to take cues about whether or not students wanted to be acknowledged outside the office.

Still another factor related to the college setting concerned dress. Staff found that although appearance issues could be explored in long-term therapy, it was easy to alienate students by clothes which caused the therapist to be dismissed as an authoritarian establishment figure. This experience, repeated often enough, motivated staff to alter their dress in closer accordance with campus norms. Although the therapists did not attempt to dress like college students, they wore clothes that were casual and comfortable to them; as a result, they were better able to relate to the students they saw. This method of handling the problem of appearance suggests alternatives to the rigid conformity often required for social workers. Particularly when dealing with the disadvantaged in their own setting, formal business attire can create avoidable barriers between the client and the social worker.

Group Psychotherapy

In addition to individual therapy, group psychotherapy was conducted by two psychiatric social workers on campus. These groups were developed to assist students whose problems were largely in the area of interpersonal relations. Group members were encouraged to express feelings, share insights, and test perceptions with their college peers. Because of their particular social conflicts, a significant number of students derived far more benefit from the group psychotherapy experience than they could possibly have gained from a more socially limited one-to-one relationship with a therapist.

Millard Ryker (1970) states:

77

For a peer-oriented student in the throes of a situational crisis, where better to find the support so necessary to resolve it successfully than in a warm, concerned group of peers .... Peers, with whom most college students are primarily concerned, are present so he may test his interactional skills and shape his identity. Authority figures, in the persons of the therapists, are also present to lend sanction to these activities and to provide a testing ground for relations with authority figures in the student´s true environment, such as parents or college professors and deans. In summary, then, a group could provide support for the members as they meet the various inevitable crises of college life and also provide an atmosphere in which they may shape and test their emerging identities.

Careful screening of applicants played a large part in the success of the groups. This processing resulted in the exclusion of students who either lacked adequate motivation or were potentially disruptive.

Indirect Services

Social workers were extensively involved in a wide variety of training and consultation assignments. From September 1970 to June 1971, they supervised two graduate students in social work, two graduate students in vocational rehabilitation, and one psychologist with a master´s degree, all of whom received training in psychotherapy. Time spent in supervising this group of trainees had the desired results of quantitative and qualitative improvement in mental health services to City College students. In addition to traditional training in crisis therapy, conferences dealt with such issues as how best to relate to minority students in their own milieu. Minority social workers in particular were active in reaching various ethnic groups on campus, and trainees were encouraged to explore outreach possibilities. Many of these students were discouraged from seeking therapy because of the office setting and procedures, even though they involved no waiting list or eligibility requirements. Often these contacts were effective stepping stones to more formal and intensive office contact between the minority social workers and students.

The general visibility of the social workers was a necessary key to encouraging minority students to utilize the mental health service. It was found that "informality and professionalism can be extremely compatible, and indeed more penetrating than the usual formally structured therapist-client interaction (Davis and Swartz, 1972). This approach, involving contact with students in

78

their own milieu, generated an increase in Black student intake from 9 per cent of the total intake in the period from January to March 1970 to 23 per cent during the period from May to June 1970.

Social workers proved adept at relating to the college as a whole. They offered consultation to faculty and administrators who requested information or advice about dealing with student mental health needs. Faculty members were able to utilize information and suggestions on how to modify teaching techniques, for example. In some instances when instructors were at a loss to know how to deal with an overt crisis in the classroom, through consultation they were able to see the situation more clearly and approach the student with more awareness. In this way it was sometimes possible to avert formal treatment. This goal was consistent with the indirect method of helping as many students as possible while minimizing the number of patients. In those instances when instructors were involved with students whose problems were too serious for the faculty member to handle, they were often relieved to be able to refer students to competent professionals, thereby avoiding problems that interfered with their academic responsibilities.

In their outreach to faculty and administrators, social workers found that education was important in removing the stigma often attached to therapy and in making psychological services a creditable part of the Student Health Services. In talking to counselors it was emphasized that students in therapy should not be treated differently from other counselees and should be given no special dispensation or privilege. In response to faculty and student interest in the Mental Health Program, social workers gave classroom guest talks which were valuable in introducing the service in its most palatable form. These talks, focusing on what constitutes mental health, often resulted in students´ relating the information to their personal lives and consequently making appointments to see the lecturer. In addition, social workers offered their services as advisors to student groups, and this outreach service was most helpful to minority organizations.

Administration of the Program

All major administrative duties were carried out by a social worker whose job it was to coordinate the Mental Health Program, assign trainees to supervisors, and make liaisons with the faculty, administration, and students. That the social worker-administrator was effective in coordinating a multidisciplinary team is perhaps reflective of a wide social perspective which can be seen as the result of a training orientation that includes components from various disciplines. Such an orientation may

well be the most eclectic in the mental health field. The
administrator was able to be responsive to the flexible and
innovative design of the program, which exacted its own type of
leadership. For instance, since the Student Health Services have
no eligibility requirements, the response of staff must be
tailored to student needs rather than to agency philosophy.
Constant evaluation of the effectiveness of the program is
necessary, especially to enable students to see a therapist as
quickly and as smoothly as possible. As Shirley Cooper (1960)
states, "The waiting period between a patient's application move
and his therapy is, in most instances, an artifact to good
therapy."

Another reason for the necessity of remaining flexible is
the endless variety of clients. Although therapists in the
program see only students, the City College population includes a
diversity of students in terms of age, background, and
sophistication about therapy. Unlike the situation at most
clinics, diagnostic categories are left wide open at the Student
Health Services.

An additional consideration involves hiring. Because of the
nature of the setting and population, it is crucial to select
staff who are appropriate and who feel comfortable at City
College, a milieu that is strikingly different from the isolated
environment of most four-year colleges and universities. Staff,
it was found, should be sympathetic to the problems of youth,
especially within the context of poverty, and should be aware of
the constant and rapid changes occurring in contemporary American
society. It is also important that staff be responsive to the
cultural and ethnic differences of City College students. This
emphasis on responsiveness might mandate certain techniques, for
example, the open-door policy used successfully by minority
social workers.

Referrals

Because of the limitations on space and staff time,
referrals were necessary if long-term therapy was indicated or if
other services such as public assistance seemed appropriate.
City College, like other community colleges, offers either
limited services, referrals, or no services whatsoever. Social
workers were particularly valuable because of their expertise in
making referrals and their awareness of social service agencies,
family service agencies, psychiatric clinics, public welfare
agencies, and private practitioners. They were often
instrumental in informing students of benefits they were not
aware of, in addition to oiling the machinery of eligibility and
entrance procedures. Thus, if the social worker saw that a

student would eventually benefit from long-term therapy, he or she would begin contacting clinics while the student was still in short-term treatment. By the time the immediate therapy ended, the student could be seen at a clinic without an interim waiting period. Such a lapse is often harmful and sometimes causes students to end treatment after only a few sessions.

Therapists felt that the referral procedure sometimes included implications of rejection for the student, especially if a therapist-student relationship had developed. Attempts were made to convey to the student the fact that the relationship could not continue for practical reasons and that the student could better meet his or her needs elsewhere. It was made clear that referrals were made for objective reasons and were related to the needs of the other students and not because the student's problems were unwelcome or because he or she had done anything to offend the therapist. The impact of referrals was minimized by having the names of people in agencies available to the student. Also, it was helpful for the therapist to inform the student of the limitations on services at the beginning of treatment.

A significant number of students came to the Mental Health Program to learn about the vocational opportunities and training requirements in the field of social work. The social worker role in the college context was seen as desirable and represented a good advertisement for the social work profession.

REFERENCES

Cooper, Shirley. Emergencies in a Psychiatric Clinic. Social Casework, Vol. 41 (March, 1960), 134.

Davis, K., and Swartz, J. Increasing Black Students' Utilization of Mental Health Services. American Journal of Orthopsychiatry, Vol. 42 (October, 1972), 771-776.

Ryker, M. Group Work with Students in a University Mental Health Health Service. Journal of American College Health Association, Vol. 18 (April, 1970), 296.

IX

OVERCOMING THE PROBLEM OF FACE-SAVING:

OUTREACH SERVICES TO CHINESE STUDENTS

Art Hom, Gerald Amada

There is an underutilization of mental health services by Chinese students at City College of San Francisco which parallels the general patterns of Chinese underutilization of community psychiatric resources in San Francisco. This article will first attempt to describe and explain some of the cultural factors which deter many Chinese students from utilizing college psychological services. This discussion will be followed by a delineation of the conceptual and pragmatic approaches which have been used by the City College Mental Health Program to overcome the cultural resistances of Chinese students to the utilization of psychological services.

Cultural Resistances to the Utilization of Mental Health Services

For the Chinese, the idiomatic expression for mental illness

or "nerves" is sun ging (神 經). Vernacularly translated, this means "spirit infested." It originates from a primitive view of the world. According to this view, man is controlled by external, mystical forces of fate; the spirits of good and evil prevail. He can attempt to ward off these evil spirits by means of ancestral worship and the close observance of a vast array of superstitious beliefs and rituals. Among those observances which are related to the maintenance of mental health is the avoidance of strong affects such as anger. Thus, one strives to ignore angry feelings, remain patient and sacrificial, turn the other cheek, and give the appearance of equanimity. Such behavior is particularly important when a person is dealing with his elders or authority figures.

Since there is little tolerance for uncontrolled emotions, there develops a social aversion to the psychologically disturbed, who are viewed as persons who have inordinately lost control of themselves. Those who suffer from sun ging are threatening to one´s family and society because they are incitive reminders of each person´s fear of losing control of his own feelings. For those who already have doubts about their own ability to control impulses, there is a dread of any association with the possessors of sun ging.

Unfortunately, the services of the college mental health program are sometimes avoided due to the fear of "guilt by association" with those who suffer from sung ging. The resistance to seeking help can be extreme. Going to a mental health clinic is, for many, an admission of being "out of one´s mind." Students then tend to wait until a crisis overwhelms them before they seek help or are brought in for assistance. In this dysfunctional state they often find it extremely difficult to maintain a sense of self-worth with which to offset their tremendous feelings of shame.

The age-old Chinese concern with "saving face" (mean gee

mun tie 面子·問題) is a primary reason for avoiding mental health services and a critical impediment to successful psychotherapy. Historically, saving face originated 2,000 years ago with the Confucian tenet of social propriety. All of man´s social behavior, according to this tenet, can be organized around and based upon one´s social position. Rulers behave like rulers, subjects like subjects. Families are headed by fathers; the wives and children must obey. The lines of authority are well defined and include all positions. Children learn their social behavior through child-rearing practices and group pressures of the family which induce shame and guilt. When a child errs, for example, fails in his academic work, the teacher blames the parents. The parents become ashamed and, to avoid any future loss of face, they shame and punish the child, according to his role and position in the family. For example, a common reprimand for an eldest son would be: "Since you are the eldest, you should be a model for your younger brothers and sisters; and since you are a son, you carry on our surname and should know better than to disgrace the family (including his ancestors)."

The problem of saving face is taught very early and manifests itself outside of the home as well, particularly in the schools. The child´s foremost responsibility (one is a child until one´s formal education is completed and one is married) is to do well in school since he obviously is not yet ready to prove himself worthy by means of assuming adult responsibilities, such as working for a living. If the child fails to fulfill his academic responsibilities, there results a loss of face for him and his family. Thus, academic failure must be avoided at all costs.

84

An additional dimension to the problem of saving face is the great emphasis placed upon psychological independence and self-reliance in the Chinese family, as demonstrated by the following example.

A nurse in the Student Health Service was called to answer an emergency in a classroom where she found a young, foreign-born Chinese man bent over with complaints of stomach pain, nausea and headache. He initially refused her assistance. The instructor had earlier noticed the student appearing ill and had unsuccessfully referred him to the Student Health Service. The student finally agreed to accept help from the nurse and compliantly followed her to the health center. Upon examination, he readily felt better and offered information regarding his history of drug abuse and the recent loss of a girlfriend. It surprised the nurse that he was so "open" and "recovered" so rapidly. She cleared him medically and referred him to the Mental Health Program in order to "talk about his problems."

The student was resistive to the referral. As he put it, the psychological approach would not work. Furthermore, the "White counselors would not understand." With much coaxing and a promise that a Chinese counselor was available, he accepted. During the therapeutic session, the student was cooperative but suspicious of being labelled mentally ill. The psychotherapist was careful to respect his autonomy and engaged the student in a mutual attempt to understand his crisis so that he could remain in control of his life. Although he was relieved to be able to speak with another Asian who could "understand what I have been through" and felt that talking was helpful, the student did not return for subsequent appointments. After the initial confusion and anxiety were alleviated, he could not tolerate the shame and embarrassment which were engendered by his psychological dependency upon the psychotherapist.

Teachers of foreign-born Chinese students frequently have considerable difficulty in encouraging their verbal participation in a classroom situation. These students are often embarrassed and awkward over their difficulty speaking English. In addition, traditional Chinese teachings admonish the student to be sensitive to the needs of the group, as opposed to his own needs; thus, he seeks to avoid drawing attention to himself by withholding his personal thoughts and feelings.

The foreign-born Chinese student is more receptive to dealing with matters which are concrete and unambiguous (such as those which commonly arise in physical science and mathematics courses). These students have particular difficulty responding to situations which require the expression of personal feelings

85

or controversial thoughts (such as commonly occur in social science courses or psychotherapeutic sessions). Their reticence to discuss personal feelings and thoughts is not due to a lack of interest, but rather is the consequence of cultural taboos which discourage psychological and social spontaneity.

Typical concerns which affect the Chinese student are whether others are genuinely interested in what he has to say and whether they might be offended by his comments. The historical origins of such self-abnegation can be discovered, for example, in ancient Chinese art. In landscape paintings, a human figure, such as a tiny fisherman, is overshadowed by vast mountains. Man is depicted as a minute part of the universe and his role is to find his humble place and live harmoniously with the world around him. The ancient cultural value placed upon humility and self-effacement often carries dilemmas for the foreign-born Chinese student who attempts to adapt to the rigors of the American college or university.

The American college as an institution values the expression of individual thoughts and feelings, much as the dominant cultural mode in this society values "free" expression of personal opinion in practically any circumstances. This, coupled with the overall societal emphasis upon individualism, presents quite a conflict for the Chinese student who has learned to devalue his personal thoughts and feelings. The Chinese student is almost "preprogramed" to do poorly in class participation and psychotherapeutic encounters. Some do struggle to change their values and behavior in the process of assimilation and in the face of academic and economic necessity.

As the Chinese student undergoes the process of assimilation from the traditional home to Western institutions and the mass media, there is a gradual learning of new values and norms. This transition can be a source of acute conflict and turmoil. Such values as assertiveness and spontaneity clash with traditional Chinese values. This explains, to a great extent, why Chinese students, both foreign-born and American-born, tend to avoid mental health services. Mental health programs are recognized as agencies which enhance the potential for assertiveness and spontaneity, and, therefore, are shunned as threats to the Chinese student's sense of cultural pride and integrity.

The Social and Economic Stresses of the Chinese Community

The Chinese word for America is gum san, literally, gold mountain, a conception which harks back to the gold rush days when the first Chinese emigrated to the United States. The dream then and now, is for economic wealth. It is the undisputed goal

86

of the Chinese student in our contemporary colleges and universities to acquire material wealth. Formal education leads to "better" jobs and "better" jobs beget improvements in one's economic status. Since the Chinese student's family frequently counts upon him to improve their own social and economic standing, he is driven by a cultural preoccupation to survive and succeed academically. Thus, academic failures such as a poor grade or non-admission to a college or university stigmatizes and undermines not only the student, but his entire family as well.

The low standard of living of recent Hong Kong immigrants who reside in San Francisco's Chinatown has been well documented. The cycle is perpetual and demoralizing. Low formal education and inadequate English-speaking abilities lead to low-income employment, substandard housing conditions and mental and physical illness. Alarmingly high rates of tuberculosis and suicide render public health officials helpless. For many of these families, poverty is an inescapable way of life; it serves only to foster even greater family and individual disorganization.

Despite this deadly spiral, almost all Chinese families believe that hard work and formal education can lead to rapid social and economic mobility. It is the American dream of rags to riches that some immigrants have realized. Those who are fortunate, have the opportunity to attend a college or university. However, many learn, all too quickly, that the goal of economic success is very far away. The demand for selective academic programs, exemplary grades and lucrative jobs exceeds the supply. To the dismay of many, the unwavering pursuit of academic and vocational goals does not solve all of one's social and emotional needs.

The single-minded pursuit of academic success is sometimes observed in certain students who force themselves to fulfill their customary scholastic responsibilities despite a recent tragic death in the family. Other students, for example, those with severe physical or psychological handicaps, develop unrealistic expectations of themselves. For example, a young Chinese male who has had a serious physical disability since childhood and a history of schizophrenia, has been enrolled in City College for five years with aspirations of becoming a physician. Despite consistently failing grades and very little aptitude for a career in medicine, he persists in his very futile academic endeavors, primarily to please his parents.

Outreach Services: Classroom Presentations

Each year, increasing numbers of students, including the

87

Chinese foreign-born, become aware of the availability of the Mental Health Program at City College of San Francisco. Generally, Chinese students tend to use the program's services only during a crisis and only after they have exhausted their personal resources, such as family, friends, etc. As indicated earlier, the number of Chinese students who receive mental health services is not representative of the number of Chinese students who attend City College. Caught between a traditional and an industrial culture while experiencing tremendous pressure to succeed and, at the same time, cope with ghetto conditions, the foreign-born Chinese are particularly susceptible to mental illness and particularly resistant to psychological help, as indicated by their low rate of utilization of mental health services.

To reach a greater proportion of the student population, particularly the "resistant" Chinese student, the Mental Health Program has relied heavily upon educational and preventative measures. The program has made extensive use of outreach services such as film workshops and student discussion groups which deal with a variety of mental health subjects, such as aggression, depression, guilt, etc.

The presentations which staff members made to classes were carried out with the prior authorization of the department chairperson and the permission of the instructor. These administrative clearances tended to give the program an "official" sanction from respected authority figures which promoted a greater acceptability for the speaker. For the Chinese student, the Mental Health Program seems less alien and less formidable when the speaker is himself Chinese. Using a variety of techniques (which will be discussed in detail later in this article), the speaker seeks to make the subject of mental health less fearful and less shameful. The classroom setting itself affords the student a sense of anonymity which protects him against feelings of self-exposure and enables him to identify with other persons in the class who are "OK" and yet express interest in the services of the Mental Health Program.

Conceptual Approaches to Reaching the Chinese Student

Based upon our clinical experience, we assume that all students have life problems or potential life problems. The more aware and informed the students are of themselves and life stresses, the more prepared they are to fend for themselves. In order to assist students in gaining self-awareness, the speaker attempts to present his facts and points of view in the most persuasive manner possible. The basic approach and attitude used are those which have also been found to be effective in brief psychotherapeutic encounters. Thomas Rusk (1971) refers to five facets of an effective therapeutic stance in crisis-oriented psychological services: calm confidence, hopefulness, active leadership, intrusiveness, and explicit empathy. These factors have been of considerable practical value to the Mental Health Program staff as they extend their services to students throughout the campus.

The importance of calm confidence is clear when one realizes that students are quick to judge whether or not a staff person is acceptable as a helping person. A role model who demonstrates genuine interest and competence can improve a student's own sense of resourcefulness and independence. The expressed confidence of the staff member in the capacity of students to develop new and exciting perspectives of themselves and the external world is often an important inspiration to many students.

When the staff representative enters the classroom or the therapeutic session, he seeks to effect psychological change by honestly conveying his sense of hope. His expectation that there can be positive results from his work can be contagious. He often must explicitly counteract the student's feelings of hopelessness which, heretofore, had been formidable obstacles to change.

Similarly, in crisis-oriented psychotherapy or in classroom presentations, there is no room for a shy, passive approach. During a classroom presentation, the psychotherapist is showing his "wares;" giving a sample of his active therapeutic style. Students want to know if they will be actively assisted. They do not want to be abandoned to a wandering, aimless struggle for self-understanding. They want and need active leadership in learning how to live their lives more creatively and assertively.

The fourth of Rusk's factors, intrusiveness, may have negative connotations for those who, like the authors, value psychological autonomy. However, when students are in crisis, they tend to develop rigid and maladaptive psychological patterns and are unable to focus clearly upon discrete aspects of their problems. This is precisely the time when the staff person must be willing to intervene in order to elicit the attention needed to exert influence upon the student. When dealing with a student who is confused or conflicted by a psychological crisis, the psychotherapist explicitly indicates that both he and the student "count" and that he refuses to accept a hopeless view of the student's emotional difficulties.

Students frequently hope that the psychotherapist not only

intellectually grasps their psychological concerns, but also has the capacity to emphathize with their emotional distress. The psychotherapist fosters a working alliance with the student based upon his readiness to reach out and acknowledge the student's emotional pain and burden. By means of his empathic acknowledgements, the psychotherapist enables the student to overcome a sense of isolation and despair.

Techniques Used to Reach the Foreign-born Chinese Student

How does one present mental health concepts in the most interesting and palatable manner to a class of foreign-born Chinese students? One technique which has been effective is the use of a few basic Chinese characters as "object lessons." Given the fact that most of the foreign-born Chinese students at City College have received some formal education in Hong Kong, this group, for the most part, reads and writes the Chinese language proficiently.

The staff member who speaks to a class of foreign-born Chinese students in their native tongue is able to establish rapport with them almost immediately. Students are pleased to be able to demonstrate their command of the Chinese language, especially when their linguistic and writing skills surpass those of the guest speaker from the Mental Health Program. The speaker's imprecise pronunciations give the students a chance to teach him something important; thus, a give-and-take relationship is initiated. The speaker is then given a significant opportunity to demonstrate how to overcome a personal deficiency. Without embarrassment he asks about the impreciseness of his pronunciations and freely and gladly welcomes the students' advice and corrections of his speech. His manner and verbal replies indicate that there has been no "loss of face." The students can quickly infer that they need not be threatened by his presence and that he and the students can fruitfully learn from one another.

Their literacy in the Chinese language enables these students to understand the etymology, meanings and usages of many Chinese characters, some of which beautifully demonstrate mental health principles. For example, the Chinese characters which

denote a "crisis" are 危機 (gui gay). The first character 危

signifies "danger." The second character 機 (gay) symbolizes "opportunity." These two characters, used in combination with each other, contain a good degree of psychological wisdom. They illustrate the sound principle that a psychological crisis is a state provoked when a person faces a threat or danger to important life goals; however, this same state of disequilibrium is also an opportunity to learn more adaptive methods of coping with personal change and stress. This useful illustration enables the student to better understand the nature of psychological crises and to appreciate the potential for recovery and growth which is inherent in personal states of crisis.

Another psychological concern which can be graphically illustrated with the use of a Chinese character is that of suicide. Originally, most characters portrayed a literal picture of the phenomena which they represented. In the case of suicide, the character which denotes danger, (gui), is again significant. When one looks at segments of this character, it is possible to

first perceive a cliff $\int$, and then a man on the edge of a

cliff, $\overrightarrow{)}$, who appears to be dangerously close to jumping or falling off (Gorden Lew, Eileen Meehan). The dramatic quality of this character tends to evoke strong emotional reactions in students. By using the metaphor of the "person on the edge of a precipice," the speaker attempts, in a general way, to discuss the students' reactions to the character and to place those reactions within the framework of what he knows about frightening or self-destructive feelings. He takes this opportunity to offer students his theoretical understanding of the dynamics of suicidal emotions. He also imparts his hopeful attitude that such feelings can be effectively managed and transformed into positive strivings, with the benefit of self-awareness (and perhaps psychotherapy).

Mental health services that work with Chinese students must be sensitive to their cultural resistances to psychological interventions. Chinese students who perceive such programs as respectful of their cultural concerns and values will utilize these services more willingly. Educational activities such as classroom presentations by Chinese staff members is one method which has proven effective in enabling many Chinese students to perceive the City College Mental Health Program as a non-threatening and beneficial psychological resource.

REFERENCES

Rusk, T. Opportunity and Technique in Crisis Psychiatry. Comprehensive Psychiatry, Vol. 12, No. 3 (May, 1971), 249-263.

Special thanks to Gordon Lew and Eileen Meehan for their assistance in the preparation of this paper.

91

X

THE BLACK PSYCHOTHERAPIST AS ETHNIC SPECIALIST:

MYTH OR REALITY?

Sam Edwards, Jr.

Introduction

The violent social upheavals of Blacks in the 1960´s and in the early 1970´s were a catalyst for moderate, but observable changes in the policies of some academic institutions and in the attitudes of many Blacks. In response to the various pressures evolving from the racial unrest, numerous American colleges and universities instituted "new" practices. To varying degrees, they recruited Third World, disadvantaged students and provided them with financial aid and "special" programs such as tutorial and counseling services. The increasing enrollment of minority college students was accompanied by the hiring of Third World college personnel in greater numbers, albeit not usually in proportion to the enrollment of minority students. As an institution with an open door admissions policy, City College of San Francisco was among those colleges which established programs to specially serve the needs of lower income and other minority students (Leavitt and Curry, 1973).

Offering an analysis of the upheavals of the mid-sixties and early seventies, Black psychoanalyst Pinderhuges (1973) stated that we should view the massive expressions of hostility against Whites as simply a stage in a process of group formation by Blacks. The various ethnic groupings which have emerged on the City College campus tend to support Penderhuges´s interpretation. Unlike the period which preceded the racial uprisings, when many Black students and Black personnel tended to eschew any affiliation with formal ethnic groupings, many Blacks now demonstrate strong ethnic allegiances. For example, Blacks can now be observed to freely offer ethnic greetings, wear natural hairstyles, and possess and avidly read books and magazines by Black American and African authors.

One sees other expressions of intragroup alliances amongst Blacks. Black students have sought out and enrolled in classes of Black instructors, who have incorporated ethnic content into their lectures and seminars. Willie Thompson, a Black sociologist at City College, has observed that a tacit consensus exists amongst Black personnel concerning the underrepresentation of Afro food in the campus cafeteria. Conversations between Black personnel have typically included references to their mistrust of White administrators and faculty. Moore and Wagstaff (1974) found that Black staff members on predominently White college campuses generally mistrust their White colleagues. "...so ingrained is the suspicion and so real the past inequities that when a Black does find a White who cares about him and respects him, it is a trauma for him." On the City College campus, increased racial pride, coupled with a degree of mistrust of Whites, has encouraged Black faculty and administrators to be more assertive in pursuing their professional and personal objectives. For example, Black faculty have increasingly participated on the Academic Senate and have organized a Black professional organization in the community college district.

Because racial and ethnic schisms exist on the campus, segments of the Black staff interact with several so-called academic communities: the dominent White community, the Black community, and the community of other ethnic minorities. Black professionals appear to be expected, by the college, to address and resolve the problems of Black students in particular, as well as to provide services for non-Blacks. As a result, some Black personnel see themselves as "guardians" of the Black student. In a nationwide study of Black educators in predominently White colleges, Moore and Wagstaff found that the majority of their respondents who taught and worked with Black students reported that they felt the need to give Black students special encouragement and emotional support. My impression is that, while Black staff at City College have, to varying degrees, internalized the expectations of the dominant White academic community regarding Blacks, some have also incorporated the values of self-help, intragroup support and cooperation, and personal assertiveness, which have been championed by Black freedom movements. Informal observations have indicated that many Black students "expect more" attention and concern from Black personnel than they do from White professionals.

Relevant Literature

The literature which deals with the roles of Black professionals in predominently White academic institutions is meager. Davis and Swartz (1972) discussed some of the roles of a Black mental health worker at City College of San Francisco. He

93

was described as follows: (1) An outreach worker, (2) a public relations person for the Mental Health Program, (3) a model for Black students, and (4) a psychotherapist. Davis asserts that a minority staff member has a special background and knowledge which enable him to be "attuned to" the minority student.

In describing his experience as a resident in a "White" psychiatry training program, Lawrence (1972) made the following point: Black trainees are expected to be instant experts on all other Blacks. Lawrence conveyed that he felt a special obligation to learn to work effectively with Blacks, even though he was trained "White."

Leavitt and Curry discussed an innovative mental health program designed to train minority professionals to function in service roles with minority students. The design of the program was influenced by "the conviction that minority students would feel more comfortable with minority staff and by the belief that minority staff would have a unique perspective to contribute to the development of a relevant program for minority students. The trainees were supervised by both a minority and non-minority staff member. The authors concluded that minority college students frequently establish a better working relationship with minority trainees than with more experienced White staff.

Moore and Wagstaff found that Blacks who hold positions as faculty, administrators and counselors in colleges "must always deal with Blacks." While Black faculty and administrators tended to be concentrated in the ethnic studies and in the special programs for disadvantaged students, Black counselors were generally working in special counseling projects for minorities. Black administrators were typically serving in the role of "Assistants to." Black personnel served in the following roles: (1) recruiters of Black students, (2) translators of Black student behavior, (3) liaison workers between the White college and Black community, and (4) problem solvers for Black students. The researchers felt that such roles were legitimate if they helped the institution to better understand the students and to provide better services for them.

Selected Roles of the Black Therapist

This section discusses two roles of a Black mental health worker in the Mental Health Program of City College of San Francisco. Particular attention will be given to the roles of a campus-wide "crisis-intervener" and of a more office-based "psychotherapist." Emphasis will be placed upon the fact that while the two roles provide significant services to the institution and to Blacks, they engender occupational stress in

94

the Black worker.

Like other members of the program, the Black psychotherapist assumes a variety of professional roles. They include: (1) psychotherapist practicing short-term, crisis-oriented psychotherapy, (2) outreach worker, and (3) crisis-intervener throughout the entire campus. What distinguishes the Black therapist´s professional experiences from those of his non-Black colleagues are: (1) his clientele, which include Black students, Black and White personnel concerned with Black students, and other non-Blacks; (2) the clientele´s perception of him as a "race and ethnic expert" because of his racial and ethnic background; (3) the therapist´s special commitment to serving Blacks; and (4) the emotional and occupational stress which accompanies his particular roles and priorities.

The Black Psychotherapist as "Crisis-Intervener"

Periodically, Black students or Black non-students have exhibited bizarre emotional symptoms which have triggered crises in classrooms or elsewhere on campus. Black or White personnel have frequently responded to these crises by requesting assistance, generally from a Black staff member or from the Black mental health worker. The more erratic and incomprehensible the student, the greater the likelihood that staff members will seek assistance. Often, however, some Black staff members have attempted to help the distressed Black student before calling the therapist, apparently because they have not attributed psychopathological meaning to the student´s behavior. Some White staff members have been observed to call for mental health consultation, or to refer troubled students sooner than the Blacks, who rarely gain assistance from White personnel when the crisis is centered around Black students. It has been repeatedly observed that when Black professionals have requested the services of the Black therapist, they seemed to expect him both to "resolve" the crisis and to enable the disturbed Black student to remain in school. On the other hand,. it appears that White professionals tend to prefer that the disturbed Black student be removed from the school because of the problems arising from the crisis.

The Black therapist, in the role of crisis-intervener, senses the sentiments of both the so-called "Black community" and "White community." While attempting to act in the best interests of the Black student, the Black therapist may make decisions which are unpopular with either Blacks or Whites. The possibilities of incurring disfavor from either source add a burden to what may already be a difficult, fear-evoking task. The following two vignettes illustrate the kind of crisis situations that induce stress in the Black therapist.

Case 1. Mr. J., a Black staff member, received a telephone
call from a White instructor who reported that a Black male
student who seemed to be emotionally disturbed was impeding
the progress of his class. Mr. J. referred the caller to
the Black psychotherapist. Mr. J. alerted the latter to the
referral, and provided background on the situation. Mr. J.
had inquired about the behavior of the student in other
classes and had learned that the student was getting along
satisfactorily in the class of a female instructor. The
more Mr. J. talked, the more evident it became that he was
skeptical of the White instructor´s report. He asked the
therapist to look into the problem if the instructor should
request the services of the therapist. The instructor did
telephone the Black therapist, asking him to visit a class
of his to observe and make some suggestions about the
student under discussion. He indicated that some of the
other students in the class had begun missing sessions
because they were afraid of this particular student.

Feeling a sense of obligation to assist in the matter, the
therapist observed the student in that classroom setting.
Approximately 25 years old, and well built, the student
seemed floridly psychotic. Along with bodily twitches, he
communicated with esoteric, abstract ideas and believed that
he had a special connection to God and to powerful men such
as Elijah Mohammed. Although in reality unable to
comprehend the concepts of "debits" and "credits," he
maintained that only he understood their real meaning.

The Black therapist recommended that procedures be initiated
to excuse the student from school and asked his parents to
hospitalize him. It was learned from the student´s parents that
the student had had numerous hospitalizations. It is important
to note that neither the White nor the Black staff member had
begun proceedings to obtain a medical leave of absence for the
student. The Black staff member was fond of the student, whom he
had known before the student had become seriously disturbed. He
had commented on the student´s superior intellectual and athletic
potential. The Black staff member was also among those Blacks on
the campus who demonstrated a strong interest in the academic
success of Black students. He seemed unable to discern the
magnitude of the student´s psychological distress and appeared
not to recognize the need for securing a leave of absence for the
student. The White staff member, although seemingly wanting to
get the student out of the classroom, also failed to take
effective action in behalf of the student. It is plausible to
assume that he may have feared arousing hostile reactions from

96

some of the Black staff.

While his intervention led to the resolution of the crisis in the classroom, the Black therapist sensed that the respective expectations of the Black and of the White staff members were quite different. The former was not convinced that the student should be removed from class, and the latter seemed to want the student to leave. The therapist felt as though he could alienate some Black staff members with his recommendation of withdrawal from college and hospitalization.

Case 2. A minor crisis arose in a recreation area of the of the campus. A White staff member working in that area telephoned a White administrator for assistance. The administrator asked the Black therapist to intervene. He explained that a Black non-student was creating some problems on campus and thought that perhaps he should not remain on the premises. Allegedly, the man, who visited the campus periodically, had already "picked up" a couple of purses of students. The White staff member seemed to have preferred the intervention of the Black mental health worker to that of the campus police.

Upon reaching the designated location, the therapist was both surprised and relieved to find the man who had precipitated the crisis sitting peacefully at a table sipping coffee. He was approximately 55 years of age, about 6'2", and weighed around 230 lbs. While one may have imagined him to be capable of violence, the man was most cooperative. He did seem emotionally disturbed, but agreed to leave the campus after a brief, cordial discussion with the therapist.

Case #2 illustrates the expectations and misperceptions which many Whites hold toward Black therapists. The Black therapist tends to be seen as the one who can handle "stereotypically" dangerous Blacks. A major worry and source of anxiety of the Black therapist is that he may not, in all instances, meet such expectations of Whites. Simultaneously, he harbors concerns that fellow Blacks may frown upon such interventions, seeing him as a "company man." However, as a crisis-intervener, the Black therapist provides invaluable services, although the role is one which can engender great stresses in him.

There were instances of Black students who experienced rather severe emotional distress in encounters with Black personnel. Often, this situation had major implications for the Black therapist. Some of the Black staff members rarely

97

associated academic problems with the emotional turmoil of Black students. Many believed that Black students "can make it" when they try. That students may be experiencing some internal conflict appears to be among the last thoughts which some Black staff members consider. It has appeared that the more actively committed the Black staff members are to assisting Black students, the more likely they are to deny the extent to which the students' academic performances may be impaired by emotional problems. When some of them do request consultation with, or refer students to, the Black therapist, they appear to want the therapist to collude with their denial.

The following two cases illustrate this point. A Black staff member was meeting with a Black student in his office. The two of them had met previously. The Black professional sensed that the student may have been emotionally upset and asked the student to visit the therapist. However, when discussing the student with the therapist prior to the referral, the staff member elaborated on the respectable grades which the student had earned. Recently, the student's grades had begun to suffer. Nevertheless, the staff member did not seem to connect the student's suffering grades with the suspected emotional problems of the student. The student came directly to the office of the therapist. Immediately, the student began describing himself as an electronic technician with plans to construct a giant, complex television and computer. He talked of men who had intercourse with his girlfriend, and of people wanting to trap him. One got the impression of acute paranoia. After making a few inquiries, the therapist learned the student had dropped out of his psychotherapy a short time ago. He was advised to return to his therapist immediately and to seriously consider taking a break from school. The student did both.

Another vignette will further clarify the point here. Mrs. F., an attractive 32-year-old Black welfare mother and one of many students in a "special program," was referred by a Black counselor in that program. She met with the Black therapist for three sessions. Before seeing the therapist, she had met periodically with her counselor. Since the new semester had begun, she had been experiencing excruciatingly painful feelings accompanied by thoughts that she would go crazy if she did not take a leave of absence from school. She explained that her counselor "is nice" and "wants me to stick with the program." She felt -- and correctly so -- that she had been referred to the therapist with the expectation that he would help to convince her to stay in school.

During the three sessions, it became evident that the student was experiencing acute anxiety reactions in the school setting. She was unable to concentrate on academic work and felt that she "had to get out of school for now." She had begun wearing a scarf tightly around her neck from which she derived a feeling of partial relief. Because she was becoming increasingly debilitated by mounting anxieties, the therapist supported her decision to leave school. He also referred her to a local mental health program.

These two cases illustrate the point that some Black staff members seem to think that "too many" Black students are "blowing" good educational opportunities. As a result, these Black professionals may not discern signs of severe emotional problems and their debilitating effects in Black students. Therefore, the Black mental health worker must quickly and accurately assess psychological crises and base his clinical decisions upon an independent assessment rather than on loyalties to either White or Black colleagues.

The Black Worker in the Role of Psychotherapist

As a psychotherapist practicing crisis-oriented and extended psychotherapy, the Black mental health staff member assumes the following roles: (a) "Black ethnic specialist" in the treatment of Black students, and (b) general pscychological counselor to all students, irrespective of their ethnic affiliation. Based upon the sources of many student referrals to the Black psychotherapist, one may infer that some campus personnel perceive him as an ethnic specialist. While a few of the Black students who seek mental health services specifically request therapy with a non-Black professional, others request to see a Black clinician. However, the preponderance of Black students seen by the Black therapist are referred by Black personnel (faculty, counselors, and clerical workers), by the nurses and clerical staff working in the Student Health Service, and by White personnel who know the Black therapist particularly well. Thus, each academic year the Black therapist tends to see proportionately more Black students than do his colleagues.

Although providing services to members of his own ethnic group is professionally and personally rewarding, it also tests his talents and "emotional strength." Like many of those who refer Black students specifically to the Black therapist, an increasing number of the Black students who request treatment with the Black therapist perceive him as a person who "understands" them or "knows where I'm coming from" better than the White therapists. Although they are interested in gaining assistance from the Black therapist, Black students frequently manifest various negative reactions to formal therapeutic arrangements and to the "therapeutic stature" of the therapist.

As with all students who initially come to therapy, many Black students, even when motivated by ethnic consciousness to obtain assistance from a Black therapist, respond quite apprehensively to the therapeutic milieu. Some even feel that the therapist can "see" their thoughts; they are guarded and cautious about disclosing intimate personal details relevant to the therapy. While recognizing that both client and therapist are Black, Black students often feel that some information is simply "no business" of the therapist. They sometimes seem to strive to avoid elaborating on thoughts and experiences.

For example, Mrs. V., an ambitious and determined Black mother of three young children, saw the therapist for three out of six scheduled sessions; she missed alternate appointments. In the first session, she reported feeling as though she were about "ready to blow up." She felt "bad" about coming to see a professional and had tried to avoid seeking help. Her mother taught her to never tell "your business" to strangers. Occasionally, when feeling desperate, she would talk over her problems with an elderly Black woman with whom she worked. She noted that she was glad that the therapist was Black. She explained that he could understand "what I'm going through." Essentially, she felt that she was too passive in her relationships with her husband and employers, and tended to turn to her domineering mother for emotional support. She felt depressed and feared asserting herself. Mrs. V.'s behavior in the therapeutic situation was significant. One sensed that she deliberately withheld relevant details. She avoided all discussion about the sessions which she missed, as well as those to which she frequently came late by 15 to 20 minutes. It seemed important to her to remain in control of the therapeutic situation.

In another case, Ms. T., an overweight, 26-year-old single student, whose aspiration was to become a teacher but who had psychologically related reading problems, was in treatment for nearly 20 sessions. She came to most of her sessions ten minutes late and when depressed she would cancel appointments because, "I didn't feel like coming." Efforts to facilitate discussion of her psychological resistances to therapy were met with obstinacy and a cool, sullen toughness. She would explain that she did not see any sense in talking about missed sessions. "I'm not going to talk about it, either," she would retort. Here the therapist would tell her that she was afraid of him and that she felt that she had to be as strong as she perceived him to be. When accurate, such interventions had the effect of allaying some of the student's fears.

Another interesting phenomenon that the author has observed

100

is the therapy dropout pattern of Black students. This writer has observed that Black males in treatment with him often fail to return after the first one or two sessions. Black female students, on the other hand, generally remained for extended therapy, although a few terminated after the third session. A number of writers (Overall and Aronson, 1963; Flowers, 1972; Sue, et al., 1974; Gibbs, 1975) have commented upon this phenomenon.

This writer has observed that a positive intense rapport sometimes developed between the Black client and himself, although many Black students interacted with the therapist in a sibling-like, rivalrous manner. For example, some responded to the therapist´s silences with silence. Grier and Cobbs (1968) elaborate on this pattern of interaction between Blacks, in social and informal settings: "The bickering, the sniping ... often said to characterize Black people in their relationships with each other seem so very much to be the rivalry of siblings. Underlying it is the feeling that ´you´re no better than I.´" This pattern was very evident to this writer. Black clients sometimes articulated thoughts that the therapist regarded himself as better than they because he was the therapist. While Black students also tended to see the therapist as "no better than me" and recognized similarities between themselves and the therapist, White students often perceived the Black therapist as inferior to themselves and readily discerned differences between themselves and the Black therapist. Many Black students, when encouraged to talk about anything which happened to be on their minds, protested by saying, "You tell me what you´re thinking, and I might tell you what I´m thinking." Black students seemed to find it very important to behave "as if" they were at least as strong and "as together" as the Black therapist appeared to be to them.

Based upon this writer´s impressions, the majority of Black students seen in therapy came at points of psychological crisis. These crises were often precipitated by underlying emotional problems. For example, the Black male students generally suffered from moderate to severe paranoia. Black female students commonly manifested moderate or chronic depression and were often involved in destructive social relationships. Both the Black males and the Black females had fears associated with academic performance.

Most of the Black students this therapist saw had one or more of the following grueling background experiences: separations between parents, punitive parents, parents with emotional and alcoholic problems, occupational instability, etc. The background experiences of these students inevitably found expression in repeated crises. For this therapist, and perhaps

101

for others, establishing a predictable, cooperative working alliance with many of the Black students constituted a major therapeutic accomplishment. Even when the therapist provided extended therapy to certain Black students, it was difficult to foster a good therapeutic atmosphere in which those students could develop a trusting relationship. The fears of trusting the therapist were pronounced.

However, an increasingly trusting relationship was important in facilitating the students´ constructive identifications with the psychological attitudes of the therapist and in enabling them to apply such attitudes toward the goal of self-examination. It appeared, however, that Black students often attempted to establish a racial, sibling-like alliance with the Black therapist, as opposed to a working or therapeutic alliance. (For a discussion of the concepts "working alliance" and "therapeutic alliance," see Greenson, 1972 and Langs, 1974.)

There is a paucity of data which deal with the Black patient-Black therapist dyad. Jones, et al. (1970) observed that the diagnostic and initial treatment process (with Blacks) requires sufficient empathy so that meaningful engagement occurs rather than a mutual and premature decision be made to terminate further therapeutic involvement. These authors also maintained that "White" psychiatric training programs are failing to prepare Black (or White) psychiatrists to address themselves to the psychological needs of Blacks. Flowers illustrated how psychiatric patients from the lower socioeconomic class tested her patience and ingenuity with significant lateness and missed appointments. Calnek (1970) described the effects of traditional psychosocial pressures upon the relationships betweeen Black patients and Black therapists. He expressed the belief that Black therapists generally have greater success with Black clients than White therapists.

Many Black clinicians will probably agree that the relationship between the Black patient and the Black therapist is highly emotionally charged. The Black patient often evokes powerful feelings in the Black therapist; moreover, it sometimes becomes tempting to explain the Black patient´s behavior on the basis of stereotypical views of his racial and cultural background. In crisis-oriented therapy, which often requires the therapist to make quick and accurate clinical decisions based upon relatively little information about the patient, one finds it too easy to fall back on cultural assumptions and stereotypical explanations. Consequently, the therapist may inadvertently steer the patient into talking about racial problems at junctures in the therapy when such discussion is contraindicated. Few can deny that racial insults are daily realities that may precipitate emotional disorders and challenge the pride and esteem of most Black people. While the oppression of racism may have devastating effects upon the individual Black patient, the therapist must be acutely sensitive to how much this particular issue should be stressed at specific points in the therapeutic process.

Other factors contribute to the unique, emotionally charged relationship between the Black patient and Black therapist. The Black therapist commonly experiences irrational (countertransference) fears of the Black patient. He often begins the treatment of Black patients with greater anxieties than he feels with their White counterparts. Along with other concerns, the Black therapist fears that Black patients will object to his authority. Because of color, ethnic, and social similarities between them, the Black therapist may easily see Black patients as "brothers" and "sisters." The Black therapist often feels a sense of intimate closeness with the Black patient. At the onset of therapy, the social and emotional distance between the Black patient and Black therapist often feels, to the latter, to be far shorter than that which exists between the Black therapist and White patient. As a result, the relationship between the Black therapist and the Black patient can easily deteriorate into an unconstructive "social affair" or into a meeting between two "siblings," unless this clinical issue is understood and skillfully handled by the therapist.

There is another burden which impinges upon the already emotionally charged Black patient-Black therapist relationship. The burden is inherent in the patient's perception, based largely upon the therapist's blackness, that he is a specialist in the treatment of Blacks. The factor of the therapist's blackness itself frequently appears to have a positive affect upon his relationships with Black patients. However, as Contress (1969/70) recognized, the blackness of the therapist fails to automatically put the Black therapist in good stead with Black clients. The increasing number of Black patients who request and accept referrals to Black therapists, suggests that the therapist's blackness can be an asset.

One may even speculate that the therapist's blackness represents to the Black patient a familiar extension of aspects of the patient's home, despite the fact that the therapist's professional role may be quite alien to the patient. Oberndorf (1953/54) has hypothesized that in mental illness certain emotional conditions exist which often require special considerations of race, creed and color before they can be even gently touched. He suggested that special knowledge in at least two particular areas is a prerequisite for undertaking effective treatment: (a) linguistics, and (b) racial heritages. Oberndorf cautioned that possession of such knowledge by the psychiatrist does not necessarily give him the skill to apply it. However, he also maintained that "the integration of the mentally disturbed individual can best be achieved if he is treated by one of those (of his own background) who understands his motivation, rather than by one considered expert in a particular form of mental illness." This writer believes that, while there are therapeutic advantages to the therapist's blackness, skill, knowledge and professional experiences are essential. Like any therapist, the "Black one" must have the capacity for warmth, empathy and understanding. Unfortunately, his blackness does not automatically endow the Black therapist with those attributes.

Summary

Following the period of the widespread unrest of Blacks in the 1960's, City College of San Francisco has made a concerted attempt to provide a more ethnically diverse staff to meet the growing needs of its ethnically and racially diverse student population. Out of this effort, several roles have evolved which are peculiar to those professionals with minority status. The academic institution has expected Blacks to provide "special" services to Black students and general services to all students. Many of the Black professionals are particularly committed to providing assistance to Black students.

These changes have significant implications for the Black psychotherapist working in the Mental Health Program on the campus. In addition to the important clinical and theoretical issues which are raised by these developments, it is clear that they frequently lead to expectations of the Black therapist which cause him considerable occupational stress. Nevertheless, the professional work of the Black therapist is a gratifying challenge to him, and his contribution to the welfare of the college is inestimable.

REFERENCES

Calnek, M. Racial Factors in the Countertransference: The Black Therapist and the Black Client. American Journal of Orthopsychiatry, Vol. 40, No. 1 (Jan., 1970).

Davis, K., and Swartz, J. Increasing Black Students' Utilization of Mental Health Services. American Journal of Orthopsychiatry, No. 42, No. 5 (Oct., 1972).

REFERENCES (Cont.)

Flowers, L. K. B.   Psychotherapy: Black and White. Journal of the National Medical Association, Vol. 64, No. 1 (Jan., 1972).

Gibbs, J. Use of Mental Health Services by Black Students at a Predominently White   University: A Three Year Survey. American Journal of Orthopsychiatry, Vol. 45, April, 1975), 430-455.

Greenson, R. The Technique and Practice of Psychoanalysis, Vol. 1. New York: International Universities Press, 1972, Chapter 4.

Grier, W., and Cobbs, P. Black Rage.   New York: Basic Books, 1968, p. 105.

Jones, B. E.   Problems of Black Psychiatric Residents in White Training Institutes. American Journal of Psychiatry, Vol. 127, No. 1 (July-December, 1970), 801.

Langs, R. The Technique of Psychoanalytic Psychotherapy, Vol. II. New York: Aronson, 1974, pp. 211-225.

Lawrence, L. E.   On the Role of the Black Mental Health Professional. American Journal of Public Health, Jan. 1972, p. 58.

Leavitt, A., and Curry, A.   Training Minority Mental Health Professionals. Hospital and Community Psychiatry, Vol. 24, No. 8 (Aug. 1973), 543.

Moore, W., Jr., and Wagstaff, L. M. Black Educators in White Colleges. San Francisco: Jossey-Bass, 1974.

Oberndorf, C. P.   Selectivity and Option for Psychiatry. American Journal of Psychiatry, Vol. 110 (1953-54), 754.

Overall, B., and Aronson, H. Expectations of Psychotherapy in Patients of Lower Socioeconomic Class. American Journal of Orthopsychiatry, Vol. 33 (1963), 421-430.

Pinderhuges, C. A.   Racism and Psychotherapy. In Willis, C. V., Kramer, B. M., and Brown, B. S. (Eds.), Racism and Mental Health (Contemporary Community Mental Health Series). University of Pittsburgh Press, 1973.

REFERENCES (Cont.)

Sue, S., et al.   Delivery of Community Health Services to Black
and White Clients.   Journal of Consulting and Clinical
Psychology, Vol. 42, No. 6 (1974), 794-801.

Vontress, C.E.   Cultural Barriers in the Counseling Relationship.
Personnel and Guidance Journal, Vol. 48 (1960-70), 13.

The writer is grateful to Willie Thompson, Andrew Curry and
Margaret Edwards for their editorial assistance with this
paper.

XI

MENTAL HEALTH CONSULTATION ON THE COLLEGE CAMPUS

Gerald Amada

The City College of San Francisco Mental Health Program (MHP) began as a pilot project designed to offer short-term, crisis-oriented psychological services to students. Since its inception in January, 1970, over 6,000 different students have been provided approximately 15,000 hours of individual and group psychotherapy. In addition, staff psychotherapists have been extensively involved in a wide variety of training and consultation services.1

The primary and most obvious purpose of an on-campus mental health program is to provide direct psychological services to students. A second and broader purpose of such a program is to effect attitudinal and institutional changes within the college that will be conducive to the psychological well-being of students.

This article will describe specific activities of the MHP that have been undertaken principally for the purpose of effecting psychologically beneficial changes in the educational environment. The pursuit of this "social" goal is predicated upon the supposition that campus-wide improvements in the delivery and quality of educational services will ultimately foster the mental health of students and, consequently, preventively render the direct use of formal psychotherapeutic services unnecessary for many students. As Whittington has suggested, within the college setting, "the faculty and administration (and the classified staff) may play an influential role in determining the vicissitudes of personality development in the college student. For this reason, it is particularly crucial to provide ongoing services of interpretation and to attempt to make mental health endeavors a mutual and

Reprinted with permission from the Journal of American College Health, Vol. 31, No. 5, April 1983.

collaborative venture between the administration, the faculty and the mental health specialists."2

Each semester a staff member of the MHP meets with classes of the police science department. Police science students are vested with legal authority and responsibility for on-campus law enforcement and, therefore, are regularly involved in dealing with disruptive and antisocial students, many of whom are seriously emotionally disturbed.

The staff therapist provides both a theoretical and practical orientation to the problems of the mentally ill student. Police science students receive dynamic insights into the behavior of the emotionally disturbed individual. In addition, they are familiarized with a range of practical strategies for dealing humanely with disruptive behavior. Finally, and very importantly, they are encouraged to enlist the assistance of the MHP in coping with on-campus psychiatric emergencies. The value of these orientations has been clearly manifested in the enhanced sophistication and humaneness with which police science students have responded to psychiatric emergencies and in their readiness to closely collaborate with the MHP staff in resolving on-campus crises.

Within the last year the services of the MHP were utilized by the Radiologic Technology Department in order to evaluate that department's procedures for interviewing students who applied for enrollment. A staff therapist was allowed to observe the interviews conducted with student candidates and requested to suggest improvements in the current procedures. Following a period of observation and analysis, the staff therapist met with a team of radiologic technology instructors. Recommendations for refining and standardizing criteria for admission were imparted and discussed. The faculty were also assisted in considering methods for restructuring the interviews (for example, providing greater privacy to interviewees) in order to gain a more objective assessment of student candidates. Although the recommendations which evolved out of these consultations have not yet been extensively implemented, the radiologic technology faculty anticipate that they will eventually lead to improved admissions procedures and higher rates of admissions of academically suitable students.

For several semesters a staff therapist has lectured to a class in the college engineering department. Since most of the students in this class would soon be entering the corporate sector of the economy, their instructor arranged a series of lectures to acquaint them with the psychology of corporate organizations. Particular emphasis was placed upon identifying the sources of emotional stress in industry as well as considering the various psychological means for coping with stress. Although the engineering students were certainly not immunized from future stress as a result of these lectures, many of them remarked afterward that the lectures offered them useful guidelines for dealing emotionally with the corporate environment.

A bilingual Chinese-American therapist arranged to visit classes which were attended predominantly by recent Chinese immigrants. Through the medium of the Chinese language and his psychodynamic interpretations of certain Chinese characters he was perceived by many students as an apt role model and an effective transmitter of important cultural values and psychological concepts. As a result, many of the recent immigrant students were able to overcome their traditional resistances to utilizing formal psychological services and, soon after the classroom presentations, made appointments in the MHP to see this therapist.3

The MHP has worked particularly closely with the English Department for over a decade. A staff therapist has conducted two types of lectures in this department. One type of presentation has entailed a description of the services of the MHP combined with an informal discussion of mental health issues. These presentations have afforded students an opportunity to interact directly and informally with a therapist by raising questions relevant to their psychological concerns, without having to formally undertake psychotherapy to achieve this purpose. Gaining an acquaintance with the MHP on this informal basis has served as a valuable stepping stone toward later utilization of the psychotherapeutic services of the MHP for many students.

A second type of presentation has been in response to special requests from English instructors for topical lectures. For example, a therapist has lectured on the subject of the authoritarian personality and reviewed, from a psychodynamic perspective, the play Equus and Kafka's short story The Metamorphosis. These lectures imparted psychological insights which augmented the students' understanding and appreciation of the assigned readings.

For a period of about two years a therapist served on the Student Review Board, a committee officially designated to review and evaluate students' petitions for a change of grade. In two respects the therapist's role on this committee was of considerable consequence.

First, a disproportionate number of the students who petitioned the committee for a grade change during the two-year period were seriously emotionally disturbed. Thus, it was crucial for members of the committee to be sensitively attuned to the motivations, anxieties and pain of this particular group of petitioners. The therapist serving on the committee was in a pivotal and advantageous position to use his expertise to help other committee members respond appropriately to the emotionally disturbed petitioner.

Second, the act of petitioning the Student Review Board ordinarily generated a good degree of hostility between the petitioner and the instructor whose assignment of the academic grade was being challenged. The adversary nature of their relationship frequently caused each to feel apprehensive and suspicious of the prospect of receiving fair treatment from the committee. Again, the therapist's role was of considerable importance in assisting other committee members and the "adversaries" themselves in resolving the conflicts inherent in the petitioning process.

The on-campus child-care facility was another recipient of the consultation services of the MHP. A therapist first met with an administrator of the child-care facility in order to develop a program which would be suitable to the needs of parents of children in care. Workshops were organized for the parents, with particular emphasis placed upon teaching and encouraging empathic responses in their child-rearing practices. The workshops provided parents excellent opportunities to enrich their relationships with their children.

Frequently, the MHP has been called upon to provide consultation, largely on an ad hoc basis, in unusual academic situations that required immediate intervention. For example, one of the academic departments requested a therapist to evaluate a situation involving a student who suffered from Gilles de la Tourette's disease (a form of tic; motor incoordination with echolalia and corprolalia). This disease caused the student during class to involuntarily and periodically emit a loud barking sound which distracted and annoyed his classmates. The instructor had given consideration to excluding the student, although he realized this would be a punitive and regrettable course of action.

On the basis of their consultation the therapist recommended that the instructor seek permission from the student to discuss his affliction with the class. The purpose of the classroom discussion would be to demystify and destigmatize the student's behavior and, thereby, to allay fears and misapprehensions about the nature of his episodic outbursts. The instructor was entirely amenable to the proposed plan, which he presented to the student, who eagerly opted to remain in the class during the discussion in order to share his knowledge and thoughts about Tourette's disease.

Following the discussion the student was referred to the therapist for further evaluation. He came voluntarily and, although he demonstrated no particular interest in receiving ongoing psychotherapy, he was delighted to learn that the therapist would be willing to serve as a mediator in the event that he encountered scrapes with instructors in the future. Although the overall long-range effects of this intervention are incalculable, the possibility that harsh disciplinary measures would be inadvertently used against the student was appreciably reduced.

In many human organizations a segment of the labor force which is commonly overlooked is the classified staff; e.g., clerical and janitorial personnel. To acknowledge and correct this oversight, a college administrator requested that a MHP therapist organize and develop a workshop for classified staff. The therapist first met with key members of the classified staff to plan a program which would address the special needs of this group of employees. A program was organized which featured simulated (comically depicted) work situations followed by meetings of small discussion groups. Various members of the MHP staff led the discussion groups which focussed upon methods for dealing effectively with the demands and stresses of work in a college setting. Afterward many of the participants spoke very favorably about the quality of their workshop experience.

The consultation services of the MHP have reached well beyond the physical boundaries of the City College of San Francisco campus. One of the MHP therapists has conducted regional conferences for counselors and administrators of other California community colleges. The conferences were devoted to teaching the principles and techniques of crisis-intervention. Conferees uniformly evaluated the program as excellent in equipping them with an armamentarium of crisis-intervention skills.

A staff psychotherapist has served on the California Community Colleges Chancellor's Task Force on the Emotionally Disturbed Student and was editor of its position paper. In the position paper the task force provided historical data, surveys and recommendations for understanding and coping with the emotionally disturbed community college student. The position paper was disseminated to counselors and administrators at each

111

of California's community colleges.

Two therapists of the MHP served on an earlier Chancellor's task force which formulated guidelines for developing community college student health services. The work of this task force led directly to the incorporation into the California educational codes, for the first time in the state's history, of references to crisis-intervention services as an essential component of community college student health services.

In sum, mental health consultation on the college campus constitutes a vital service to the entire academic community. Although such services will obviously neither prevent mental illness nor eliminate the need of many, even quite functional, students for formal psychological treatment, their impact in fostering an educational environment which will promote the emotional well-being of students can be far-reaching.

REFERENCES

1. Amada, G. The Paucity of Mental Health Services and Programs in Community Colleges: Implications of a Survey. Journal of the American College Health Association, June 1975, Vol. 23, No. 5, 345-349.

2. Whittington, H. G. Psychiatry on the College Campus. New York: International Universities Press, Inc., 1963.

3. Amada, G., and Hom, A. Overcoming the Problem of Face-Saving: Outreach Services to Chinese Students. In Amada, G. (Ed.), Mental Health on the Community College Campus. Washington, D.C.: University Press of America, 1978.

XII

WHY PEOPLE DISTRUST PSYCHOTHERAPISTS

Gerald Amada

A character in one of George Bernard Shaw's plays wittily remarked that all professions were conspiracies against the laity. Psychotherapy as a profession is sometimes seen in this unseemly light by the public.

There are many rational and valid reasons for the widespread distrust of the psychotherapy profession. First, many therapists are poorly trained and, therefore, lack the requisite skills and knowledge to perform their professional duties well. Second, it is hardly a secret that psychotherapists as a group are apparently as prone as the rest of the population to personality defects and mental illness. When the emotional conflicts of psychotherapists remain unresolved, their objectivity and judgment become impaired and the quality of their clinical work of course suffers as a consequence. Finally, the rich smorgasbord of diverse and contending psychotherapies that have proliferated in this country must give even the most unsuspecting observer cause for concern and skepticism. After all, if one therapy emphasizes the importance of self-insight; another, behavioral change; and yet another, emotional catharsis -- each laying claim to irrefutable success with its methods and objectives -- how is it possible to accredit one without discrediting the others?

In addition to these rather obvious reasons for mistrust, the profession of psychotherapy arouses suspicions due to a number of other, more subtle, factors, some of which involve attitudes that are not altogether rational or conscious.

Polarized Perceptions of Psychotherapists

Two quite polarized perceptions of therapists may sometimes serenely cohabit the mind of a single individual. One perception is that therapists are providing clandestine services which are designed to subvert the status quo of the individual and society. At this end of the perceptual spectrum therapists are viewed as champions of sexual libertinism, irreligiosity and indiscriminate nonconformity. The policy of confidentiality which therapists maintain about their work is seen as further evidence of nefarious goings-on.

At the other end of the perceptual spectrum the psychotherapist is viewed as a rich font of miraculous cures. Therapists are endowed with the godlike qualities of omniscience, infallibility and an imperviousness to the ordinary hardships of life. A frequent offshoot of these attitudes is the expectation that therapists have "all the answers" to the human condition and can, if they would only apply their omnipotent talents, completely eliminate human suffering.

What accounts for these polarized attitudes? One explanation is that therapists are readily perceived as parental figures and, thereby, arouse strong transference or infantile reactions in others. Thus, they tend to represent either the "good," flawless parent of early infancy who succors and heals, or the "bad" parent who rejects, abandons or secretly plots mischief (sexual and otherwise).

The perception of the therapist as a "bad," conspiring parent understandably arouses distrust and suspicion. It is important to recognize, however, that the perception of the therapist as the personification of all that is good also arouses feelings of distrust. Unquestionably, a belief in the perfection of others can never be realistically fulfilled or trusted and when it is irrationally embraced as a conviction, it inevitably leads to disappointment, disillusionment and even greater distrust.

The Need for Perfection: The Emperor´s Clothes" Syndrome

In certain respects the mere existence of psychotherapists is an incitive reminder of the imperfections of society and of the human personality. Since most people prefer to minimize or conceal their imperfections, psychotherapists, by dint of their dedication to the uncovering (and understanding) of personal imperfections, are commonly viewed as relentless adversaries. They are the symbolic counterparts of the child in the fable, "The Emperor´s Clothes," who ingenuously betrays the emperor´s nakedness. Psychotherapists, as seekers and revealers of naked personal truths, threaten the very fabric of those human strivings which seek to cover and disguise imperfections.

This perception of psychotherapists leads to the fallacious belief that professional involvement with a psychotherapist is an unavoidable indication of one´s lack of personal success and

114

wholeness. If one happens to be the parent of a person who enters psychotherapy, the therapist may very well be viewed as a foe who will expose and blame the parent for his imperfections as child-rearer. In short, the quest for personal perfection can become a powerful source of distrust toward psychotherapists who, in accord with their avowed professional objectives, quest to uncover and learn about personal imperfection.

Psychological Deprivation as a Source of Distrust

Those persons who do not receive psychotherapy may develop intense ambivalent emotions toward those who do, especially if the recipient of treatment is a close friend or relative. When a member of a family enters psychotherapy, for example, other family members may react with strong feelings of deprivation as a result.

There are at least two explanations for this reaction. First, family members may experience a sense of loss and envy over the patient's willingness to share deep personal concerns with someone other than themselves. They may interpret the patient's actions, perhaps with a fair degree of accuracy, as a criticism or indictment of the quality and character of family life. In this instance it is the therapist who is envied for being the principal repository of personal information about the family.

Second, when one person hears about another entering therapy, he may quite involuntarily compare himself unfavorably to the patient. Realistically or not, he may entertain thoughts of the patient in therapy engaging in an enriching personal experience. From such thoughts may evolve feelings of deprivation, loss and rivalry toward the so-called "privileged" patient. In this instance it is the patient who is envied for being regarded as the fortunate beneficiary of a nurturing relationship. Viewed from this perspective, the therapist is unavoidably cast in the role of the "bad" parent who plays favorites, i.e., nurtures "undeserving siblings," while depriving others. This image of psychotherapists as favorers of the fortunate few and deprivers of the neglected many, easily leads to feelings of distrust toward them and their profession.

Economic Considerations as a Source of Distrust

Economic considerations sometimes play a curious role in arousing distrust of psychotherapists. When we purchase most commodities or services, whether they are refrigerators or new doors, we have a tangible idea of what such items should cost. We also have certain concrete yardsticks for measuring the quality

115

of the work or commodity purchased. If the carpenter´s door falls off the hinges or the refrigerator breaks down in a week, we can quickly and correctly decide that we have not gotten our money´s worth.

How can a person effectively apply economic principles to the experience of psychotherapy. If, for instance, a patient spends thirty dollars a week in psychotherapy, what does he have to give up in order to incur this ongoing expense? If it is an occasional dinner out or a vacation, the patient must weigh the loss of these psychologically beneficial treats against what he may gain from psychotherapy. How is this done? How will the patient evaluate in monetary terms how much increased self-esteem, greater insight, bolstered self-confidence and improved social relationships -- the potential rewards of therapy -- are worth to him?

Self-esteem, confidence, insight and self-respect are intangible qualities. Since it is impossible to put a price on or quantify these personal qualities, it is enormously difficult for most people to precisely determine, in financial terms, the potential value of therapy.

Another factor which makes it extremely difficult to precisely determine the economic value of therapy is the vagueness of the term "value." The effects of psychotherapy are multidimensional; that is, people can improve in more than one direction at a time. If, for example, a person feels more confidence as a result of therapy, but uses the self-confidence to bully others, can we truly regard the therapy as having value?

Finally, the cost-effectiveness of psychotherapy is torturously difficult to determine for the following reasons: (1) It is never possible to prove with exactitude a causal relationship between a therapist´s interventions and a patient´s psychological gains. For example, a therapist may over a period of several months encouragingly explain and reveal to a patient the many (past and current) sources of his psychological stress. Over this time the patient becomes more self-aware, confident and hopeful. Although patient and therapist alike may for good reason agree that the therapy is beneficial, realistically it will not be possible for them to identify: (a) what exactly occurred in the therapy to produce such positive results and (b) to what extent outside influences (e.g., a new love relationship) also contributed to the psychological progress of the patient.

(2) A perpetually elusive issue in assessing the (cost) effectiveness of psychotherapy is the matter of deciding when to

116

evaluate psychological change. Let us take the hypothetical example of a nineteen-year-old woman who has been treated successfully for depression over a period of ten months. Should we study her progress after five months? Or, would it be better to do this at the point of termination of therapy? Perhaps, instead, it would be more valid to assess her improvement after a lapse of ten years, at which time she may be pursuing a career and/or raising children.

In a society which has become pervasively technological and computerized, there is an increasingly widespread intolerance and suspicion of ambiguity, particularly with respect to the economic costs of human services. Since psychotherapy is an inherently ambiguous human enterprise, with a cost-effectiveness which can only approximately be estimated, economic considerations can play a major role in generating attitudes of distrust toward the professional psychotherapist.

Idealization as a Source of Distrust

As indicated earlier, the mere presence of a psychotherapist can induce powerful transference reactions in others. The psychotherapist can activate those strong infantile wishes and longings which were originally harbored in relation to one's parents. For example, it is not unusual to detect indications in many persons of a genuine conviction that psychotherapists have omniscient and omnipotent powers. A corollary of this conviction is the magical belief that those who practice psychotherapy can actually "see through" others. Naturally, such beliefs cause one to feel psychologically transparent and vulnerable in relation to therapists.

The transference attitudes which therapists animate in others sometimes cause them to be approached on an interpersonal basis as if they were larger-than-life, bounteous personages. All too often, as a result, they are treated with adulation and obsequiousness in social situations. Such treatment occasionally places social hardships upon psychotherapists who, in order to demonstrate their humanness, may feel it necessary to ostentatiously give evidence to others of their own personal doubts and weaknesses.

The tendency to idealize psychotherapists readily leads to distorted perceptions of how they lead their personal lives. For example, therapists are often thought of as having perfectly integrated personalities which are impervious to the human conflicts of everyday life. They are expected to always work and relate harmoniously with others and to respond only in an unemotional, self-controlled and ascetic manner. In other words,

117

they are expected to conduct themselves in their personal lives very much as they commonly do in their psychotherapeutic encounters with patients.

As clinical observation has clearly established, underlying and paralleling attitudes of idealization and awe are usually equally powerful feelings of (largely unconscious) contempt. The combined attitudes of lofty admiration and devaluing contempt produce interesting social reactions to the disclosure of unsettling events in the personal lives of therapists. Thus, the discovery that a therapist has committed suicide or is the parent of an emotionally disturbed child frequently causes the lay person to initially react with shock and disapppointment (loss of the ideal). This reaction is soon followed by a kind of self-righteous indignation (the surfacing of the underlying contempt) verbalized by such comments as: "Therapists think they are so smart and perfect. They have as many problems as other people. Actually, they have more problems than others. So what makes them think they can help others when they can't straighten out their own lives?"

Idealization of therapists engenders unrealistic expectations of their human capabilities and qualities. The envy that awe inspires and the inevitable disappointment which results from the discovery of a therapist's human limitations combine as strong catalysts of distrust.

The realistic and unrealistic causes for distrust of the psychotherapy profession are legion and complex. Considering the complexity and universality of these causes, it is indeed a remarkable fact that an estimated thirty-four million Americans are currently receiving psychotherapy.

XIII

DEALING WITH THE DISRUPTIVE COLLEGE STUDENT:

SOME THEORETICAL AND PRACTICAL CONSIDERATIONS

Gerald Amada

Over the last several years college personnel throughout the
nation have found themselves faced with an increasing number of
disruptive students. These are students who, through their
behavior or attitude, persistently interfere with the academic
and administrative activities of the campus. Some of these
students actively hamper the ability of other students to learn
and instructors to teach. Some even threaten the physical safety
of others and themselves.

Predictably, a disproportionately large number of disruptive
students are seriously emotionally disturbed; their emotional
disturbance being either a cause or effect of their disruptive
behavior. There are several reasons for the burgeoning numbers
of such students now attending colleges and universities:

(1) Recent legislative changes have occasioned the release
from state mental hospitals of more emotionally disturbed
patients into the local communities. For example, in California
during the past twenty years, the state's mental hospitals have
depopulated from a patient caseload of 37,000 to 3,000.

(2) Advances in the use of psychotropic medications have
helped to maintain psychiatric patients in their local
communities, thus allowing many such persons to avail themselves
of an education in a nearby college or university.

(3) Many mental health practitioners, often with good
reason, regard the college campus as a desirable and enriching
resource for their patients. Occasionally, however, the
emotionally disturbed student is ill-prepared to cope with the
rigors of college life and, in response to his own acute anxiety
and confusion, will behave disruptively in order to enlist the
assistance and support of others. This problem is frequently

119

exacerbated by a lack of collaboration and planning between the college and the referring mental health practitioner, causing the emotionally disturbed student to feel defenseless and abandoned when he arrives on campus.

The disruptive student, whether emotionally disturbed or not, often angers, baffles, alarms and immobilizes those instructors and administrators who must cope directly and immediately with the disruptive behavior. In some cases the disruptive behavior clearly warrants disciplinary action on the part of the instructor or administrator.

According to Close and Merchat (1), there are five principles relating to discipline which emerge from case law.

1. The law does not expressly prohibit a college from disciplining a student for misconduct, even when that misconduct is directly related to his/her physical or mental handicap.

2. Each college is required to provide "reasonable accomodation" to the physically/mentally handicapped. That is, major disruptions to the educational process may be met with disciplinary action, but minor disruptions need to be tolerated under the "reasonable accomodation" principle.

3. Each college is required to adopt rules and regulations regarding appropriate student behavior, spell out penalties for violation of these regulations, and clearly describe due process procedures for students who wish to appeal these penalties. The formal policy statement of the college should, therefore, provide a wide range of sanctions so that there is a series of alternatives to deal with the disruptive behavior of students. Alternatives for minor disruptions should include efforts to provide assistance to the student, for example, by referring him to a mental health professional on campus if available.

4. The sole basis for imposing disciplinary sanctions on a student is that student's behavior, regardless of the etiology of that behavior. A college may not discipline a student for being "mentally ill" -- only for explicit behavior prohibited by the Student Code of Conduct. For this reason, it is extremely important that the student's exact behavior be documented in writing in accurate detail. All procedures and recommendations relating to the disciplinary process also need to be clearly documented.

5. Although mental health professionals must follow legally defined obligations to maintain confidentiality regarding client communications and records, all persons employed by a community

120

college must report serious threats or risks of harm to self or others, as well as known instances of child abuse. (This principle is based upon a section of the California education code.

When the disruptive behavior of a student threatens the welfare of other individuals and the educational institution itself, it may be necessary for the college to institute disciplinary measures. The range of disciplinary measures may include warnings, reprimands and, in the more serious cases, exclusion from certain classes or from the college as a whole.

Although most colleges have adopted a set of rules and regulations regarding student conduct, as Wagener et al. point out (2), relatively few schools have adopted detailed procedures to be followed when considering restricting the enrollment of students for disruptive behavior. Some schools do not intervene until the state laws on civil commitment or criminal behavior apply. Others regard disruptive behavior as strictly a disciplinary matter to be dealt with solely on an administrative basis.

At City College of San Francisco the Mental Health Program is utilized extensively by instructional, administrative and classified staff in trouble-shooting and resolving incidents involving disruptive students. The utilization of a crisis-intervention model which makes use of the expertise of mental health practitioners has several weighty advantages.

First, college staff who are confronted by disruptive students are frequently frightened, diffident and unclear regarding their rights and prerogatives. The mental health professional can provide staff not only with vital emotional support and empathy throughout the disruptive crisis, but can also be helpful by informing staff of their legal and administrative rights and limitations.

Second, the alarming nature of many disruptive incidents frequently causes college staff to be either overly permissive or inordinately punitive in their attempts to resolve crises. A mental health professional can be invaluable in assisting college staff to develop effective strategies and the requisite objectivity to carry out disciplinary action (if such is necessary) in an efficient and humane manner.

Third, because instructors and administrators sometimes have widely different and conflicting viewpoints regarding the causes and degree of seriousness of disruptive crises, they may each tend to favor and pursue disparate courses of action to resolve them. This can result in an acrimonious and dangerous impasse between them that serves to protract and aggravate the crisis. In instances of this nature a mental health professional can be essential in identifying the areas of disagreement, in serving as a mediator for the contending principals and, by making recommendations as to how their differences and the crisis can best be resolved.

When staff consult the Mental Health Program for assistance with a disruptive student they are usually advised to carefully document their observations and concerns. The documentation should be devoid of psychological jargon or speculation (e.g., "This person seems to be a paranoid schizophrenic" or "I think he´s on drugs"). Documentation should be specific and concise, describing exactly the disruptive and objectionable behavior that has been observed. The documentation should be immediately transmitted to the Department Chairperson and to the appropriate dean. Depending upon the gravity of the disruption, the staff member may receive recommendations ranging from issuing a warning to the student to desist from further disruptions to, in very serious or dangerous cases, immediate exclusion from class or the college. If the disruptive student seems to pose a serious and imminent danger to the staff member, the latter is given extensive advice and information regarding which administrative and/or law enforcement authorities he must immediately inform of the incident and advised also as to what precautions he must take in order to insure his own personal safety. When the disruptive student´s behavior warrants administrative intervention, the mental health professional immediately contacts the appropriate administrator in order to report the incident and to share his interpretations and recommendations regarding the matter.

When the matter has been resolved at the administrative level it is essential that the staff person who originally reported it be informed of its disposition or resolution. Without the benefit of this information, the reporting staff person is unnecessarily left on tenterhooks to wonder and worry about whether the crisis will actually be resolved.

It is understandable that staff who report disruptive students to the Mental Health Program frequently expect to resolve the crisis by referring such students for psychological treatment in the program. Although such referrals are sometimes appropriate and beneficial, in most instances they are abortive and unnecessary. There are several reasons why such referrals are usually unsuccessful.

First, the student who is referred for treatment on the

122

basis of his disruptive behavior ordinarily (and correctly) considers the referral and the therapy as a disciplinary measure and, therefore, wants no part of it. Second, the majority of seriously disruptive students have already received (and may still be receiving!) psychotherapy. Since the therapy they have already received has not yet prevented them from manifesting disruptive behavior, they surely are entitled to take less than a sanguine view of seeing yet another therapist about their "problems." Thus, in most instances, joint consultation between the mental health counselor, the staff member who is reporting the disruptive student, and the appropriate administrator -- without the direct involvement of the student himself -- is usually the preferred course of action. Naturally, the disruptive student has every right to appeal the ultimate administrative decision and to have full and direct involvement in the administrative review of his case, should he so choose.

In this author's role as a mental health consultant to some of California's community colleges and to the California Community Colleges Chancellor's Office, I have discovered that many, if not most, community colleges require that the disruptive student receive psychiatric or personal counseling as a condition of either continued enrollment or reenrollment in the college. Although this practice may, in part, be motivated by a humane recognition that the disruptive student is a victim of emotional stress (as either a cause or effect of his disruptive behavior), and, therefore, could conceivably benefit from psychotherapy, there are several reasons why this practice should be discontinued and prohibited.

1. Requiring the disruptive student to receive psychotherapy distorts and undermines the basis for corrective disciplinary action. The focus and impetus for disciplinary action is the disruptive behavior of the student, not the student's putative mental illness or disorder. When a college administrator requires the disruptive student to undertake psychotherapy he is perforce making a psychiatric judgment using psychiatric criteria. Even if he were doing this with the benefit of having first consulted a mental health professional, the requirement is being carried out by means of the administrator's authority and, therefore, he is unavoidably making a psychiatric determination. Administrators do not possess the legal right to make psychiatric evaluations and determinations of this nature. On the other hand, they most certainly do have the legal right and prerogative to determine what is and is not acceptable student behavior on their respective campuses and to carry out non-psychiatric discipline in cases of student misconduct (e.g., reprimands, suspensions, etc.).

2. The requirement of psychotherapy for the disruptive student is often motivated by fanciful and naive notions about psychotherapy itself. One such notion, for example, is the belief that once a student receives psychotherapy, his disruptive behavior will abate or cease. Although this is sometimes true, it is also true that many persons who receive psychotherapy remain disruptive and at times actually become violent, despite their psychiatric treatment.

An analagous belief is that psychotherapists have the omnipotence not only to prevent disruptive behavior, but to accurately predict disruptive recidivism. Numerous research studies as well as common sense indicate that the ability of the mental health professional to predict disruptive or violent behavior is admittedly quite limited. There are at least two reasons for this limitation: (1) The way in which a psychiatric patient thinks and behaves in the consultation room often has little relationship or carry-over to how he will behave and think elsewhere. Thus, a therapist, especially if he does not understand his patient´s state of mind well, may have an unrealistic view of his social functioning and potential for behaving disruptively. (2) No psychotherapist, no matter how sensitive or astute, can anticipate the myriad stressful circumstances which his patient may encounter on the college campus. Thus, a patient may be well fortified by his therapy to enter college, however, once there, a poor grade, a humiliating evaluation, or a long delay on the registration line, can cause the fragile patient to regress and become disruptive.

For these reasons, the common practice of requiring psychiatric agencies and practitioners to submit reports to administrators indicating their patient´s readiness to reenroll is suspect and should be stopped. This should be replaced simply with an administrative requirement that the disruptive student who is petitioning for continued enrollment or reenrollment meet with a designated administrator(s) who will inform the student that a repitition of his disruptive behavior (assuming the student is allowed to continue) will result in further disciplinary action. If a referral to an on- or off-campus mental health agency seems appropriate, the administrator can tactfully assist with such a referral, without making it a requirement.

3. Requiring the disruptive student to receive psychotherapy is unequivocally a coercive measure that serves to instill in the student resentment toward potential sources of help, i.e., the therapist and the therapy. Such students, if they conform to this requirement, will agree to see a therapist but frequently will invest no personal involvement in the treatment process

124

itself and, consequently, typically derive little from the therapy, other than the impression that psychotherapy is a punishment which must be stoically endured. It may reasonably be argued that some of these students eventually overcome their hostility and resistances and, thereby, receive some benefit from therapy that they would otherwise not have received had they not been required to be in treatment. If this is indeed true, I would argue that, considering the resentment and distrust which so frequently ensues from compulsory therapy, the price is much too high.

4. Ordinarily, for psychotherapy to work effectively, it must be conducted on a confidential basis. This is the cornerstone of psychotherapeutic treatment and is maintained in order to instill in the patient a trust of the therapist which is essential to the patient's welfare. A requirement that the disruptive student receive psyhcotherapy naturally implies that the college will be informed of the student's therapeutic activities, including perhaps his progress and prognosis. Thus, this requirement serves to contaminate and undermine the confidential therapeutic relationship and, consequently, limits the potential for success.

5. The administrative requirement of psychotherapy as a condition of continued enrollment tends to divide the authority over the student's status in the college between the college and the mental health community. In practical terms, what frequently happens is that a therapist will recommend reenrollment and the administrator will feel protected by that authoritative recommendation. In reality, that recommendation affords no protection to the administrator or the college, insofar as that student's future behavior is concerned.

The increased numbers of disruptive students attending colleges and universities have reached alarming proportions. In order to deal effectively and humanely with such students schools must establish a systematic and legally acceptable set of procedures for dealing with disruptive behavior. An on-campus mental health program can be an invaluable asset in assisting college staff in developing and implementing such procedures. (3)

REFERENCES

1. Close, C. A., and Merchat, M. M. Emotionally Disturbed
   Students: Legal   Guidelines.   Chancellor's   Office,
   California Community Colleges, 1982.

2. Wagener, J. M., et al., Reacting to the Uncooperative,
   Severely Disturbed Student: A survey of Health Center
   Policies. Journal of the American College Health
   Association, Vol. 31, No. 5 (April, 1983).

3. Amada, G. Mental Health Consultation on the College Campus.
   Journal of the American College Health Associaton, Vol. 31,
   No. 5 (April, 1983).

126

XIV

GROUP PSYCHOTHERAPY ON THE COMMUNITY COLLEGE CAMPUS

Andrea Polk, Annette R. Pont-Gwire

As co-leaders of a psychotherapy group at City College of San Francisco, we have found group to be an effective and gratifying treatment approach for students. The intent of this article is to discuss group psychotherapy on the community college campus. It will include an examination of the role of this service on campus, the process of membership recruitment, and a brief description of the selection procedure.

WHY GROUP IN THE COMMUNITY COLLEGE SETTING?

City College of San Francisco has an established mental health program that provides individual treatment including crisis intervention, brief psychotherapy, referrals, and consultation for staff and faculty. The Mental Health Program has also provided group experience for students for some years now with good results. Because of funding cutbacks in mental health services in the larger community, health facilities on the college campus are being more widely utilized. In this light, group can be effective in delivering services to more students per hour than can individual therapy. In addition, these services aid in students' academic performance and overall adjustment; accordingly, there is a direct effect on retention of students in school.

Research and practice indicate that group psychotherapy is an effective treatment approach that enhances social functioning and skills, as well as individual development (Yalom, 1970, Saretsky, 1977). In fact, in our experience, many students find that a transition from individual to group therapy is an excellent means of expanding on the insights achieved in one-on-one counseling. Many of the issues and problems that arise for students can be handled in a group setting. Among these are concerns involving social and interpersonal skills, issues arising from relationships -- both in the classroom and out -- and encompass all stages of adult development.

127

Like many community colleges, CCSF's population is particularly diverse in terms of race, and sexual orientation. Given the recent influx of Asian and Central American immigrants to the Bay Area, CCSF is especially rich in its student body makeup.

TARGET POPULATION

All community college students are eligible for mental health services. Presently, students range in age from 17 to 70, and come from highly diverse cultural and racial backgrounds. In addition to the recent immigrants and political refugees from Asian and Central American countries, diversity is further reflected by the presence of those with issues of sexual orientation, learning disabilities, as well as women recently reentering the academic world. Accordingly, selection of members for a group on a community college campus should be sensitive to the variability of the issues presented at a given college as well as the diagnostic/clinical/psychological concerns presented.

It is essential for a therapist or counselor to be sensitive and open to these issues; that is, cross-cultural factors may be as important and anxiety provoking as psychological ones. Conflicts and problems are often presented under the rubric of classroom difficulties. In the initial group screening interview, these difficulties are generally expressed as problems in concentrating, test anxiety and deteriorating academic performance. These manifest problems can obscure conflicts over relationships, self-esteem, separation, depression, social fears or sexual concerns. These concerns are all appropriate for work in a group forum. Some brief examples may serve to highlight:

John -- a 21 year old white male -- complained of difficulties concentrating in class. Although normally a good student, John found himself increasingly unable to focus on academic work. He had recently moved out of his parents' house, and was living in an apartment with roommates. He reported that he occasionally had arguments over "small things" with these roommates.

Gloria was a 30 year old Lesbian woman who sought group as a means of understanding her more and more frequent bouts of anger and depression.

A 28 year old immigrant from Mainland China, Lin was an engineering student forced to live with many relatives in a tiny downtown apartment. She brought a troubling perfectionism to her studies, and was struggling with her sense of obedience to her rigidly traditional parents, who disapproved of her emerging

128

autonomy and independence.

At 18, Raul had been sent to the United States by his family to study when the civil war in his native Central American nation intensified. A year later, as a CCSF student, the disruption of his adolescent development caused by the war, and his social isolation in a strange and new country contributed to a deterioration of his academic functioning. He came to the Student Health Service complaining of headaches, and was referred for group therapy by the school nurse.

Tran was a 22 year old Vietnamese refugee who had made her way to the United States under harrowing circumstances as a "boat person." She was now living in extreme poverty and isolation, but had recently become involved in a serious romantic relationship. Her concerns at this time involved guilt over sexual feelings and wishes.

These examples illustrate typical student complaints which lead to inclusion in group. Problems are not always confided to a health worker, but may instead be told to an academic counselor or an instructor, who, in turn, may refer the student to the Mental Health Program.

SELECTION CRITERIA

A basic assumption about group that holds true for almost every worker in the field is that group participants cannot be thrown together arbitrarily without taking into account mutual suitability, and that not every patient is necessarily able to benefit from group treatment (Mullan and Rosenbaum, 1962). While Yalom (1970) screens out severe character disorders, borderline psychotics, addicts, and alcoholics, there does seem to be a recent trend toward greater individualization and less concern for screening out a patient on the basis of his formal diagnostic classification (Leopold, 1957). Many therapists limit their selection to people of similar age. These practitioners appear to have an inhibition about mixing younger adults with older adults, and rationalize this exclusion on the basis of a separation of overlapping interests: it is feared that members will be unable to identify with each other's age-specific problems (Saretsky, 1977).

In the context of the CCSF community, the division of students into discrete categories seems artificial. We believe that background, age, and diagnostic category are not as important as interpersonal style to the outcome of group, although we do exclude severely disturbed and acting-out individuals.

In this regard, we grappled with the issue of homogeneity. On the one hand, homogeneity already existed, in that all members of the group were students. In turn, this provided a baseline for the heterogeneity of the group with respect to age, sex, and race.

We feel that group at CCSF allowed student participants from varied backgrounds to focus on common goals, enhance interpersonal growth, as well as augment interpersonal understanding, in a setting which encouraged the reworking of attitudes, preconceptions, and stereotypes.

PROCEDURES FOR GENERATING MEMBERSHIP

Practical experience at CCSF has revealed to us the emotional and social isolation that many students undergo, both in the classroom and out. Therefore, we believe that to effectively reach as many students as possible should involve a considerable outreach effort. Our plan included making the faculty, staff and students as aware as possible of the group's existence. This procedure involved two general stages: recruitment and selection. Initial contact was made with the administration and then followed by letters to college counselors, nurses, heads of departments, and faculty.

Next, we attended faculty in-service training workshops in order to describe and promote our group services.

The study body was approached more directly with announcements in the school newspaper, and flyers which were posted throughout the campus.

The recruitment process for the psychotherapy group was often slow and painstaking. However, our outreach efforts resulted in an extensive master-list of potential participants from which to select.

PROCEDURE FOR SELECTING PARTICIPANTS

The procedure for selection to group included two important functions: one entailed gathering information from applicants, and the second involved education preparatory to starting group. Whenever possible, group co-leaders interviewed prospective members jointly.

Evaluation of applicants in these pre-selection interviews assessed not only the usual information such as history, family of origin, prior treatment, and motivation, but also academic functioning and problems in school.

130

EDUCATION AND PREPARATION

Research shows that effective preparation sets the stage for group cohesiveness, low rates of attrition, and successful group outcome (Yalom, 1970). Other literature points to the fact that when a client is placed in a group situation where both his/her goals and the group goals are unclear, such situations may heighten the client's anxiety and result in premature termination (Saretsky, 1977; Whitaker and Lieberman, 1964). Further validation of the importance of group preparation has been demonstrated in laboratory research. Members have been found to be more anxious, frustrated, and defensive, resulting in early termination when the group goals, methods and expected group behavior were ambiguous. However, prepared group members had more faith in therapy and participated in more interpersonal interactions than those less prepared (Cohen, 1959; Yalom, 1970). While beyond the scope of this article, the interested reader can find a comprehensive and systematic guideline for group preparation in Yalom (1970).

What makes pre-group preparation essential on the community college campus arises, in part, out of the semester system and the time restraints imposed by this structure. In the experience of Yalom and others, the first twelve sessions generate the most resistance, and during this period members are particuarly vulnerable to leaving group. Accordingly, Yalom asks members for a commitment of at least twelve sessions to reduce dropout potential. Given that the college semester is not more than sixteen weeks, a twelve-week commitment would involve nearly the whole semester. Therefore, after consideration of our extensive pre-group preparation, a commitment of five weeks seemed to us a more reasonable ratio.

By the end of the second interview we had a reasonably good idea whether the student should be invited to join group. For those that seemed suitable, the group rules and expectations were then explained. Sufficient time was allowed for the student to ask as many questions as he/she needed before committing to join group. When everyone agreed that the student would join group, the time and place were established and word given that the student would be officially notified by a short letter.

The outcome of the overall process provided information regarding applicants' personality structure, ego functioning, and interpersonal communication skills as well as the presence of concerns deemed appropriate for group as opposed to individual therapy. (Some students were already in individual therapy but could benefit also from group. These students, who met the

interview criteria, were   accepted   for the group, and they
continued concurrently with   their   individual   treatment).
Occasionally, the screening interviews revealed the   student who
was either dysfunctional or potentially disruptive for work in
this type of group; persons such as psychotics, low functioning
borderlines, substance   abusers,   and severe characterological
types. When the   interviews   brought   such students to our
attention, appropriate referrals were made to other services
instead of to group. For example:

> Although diagnosed as a chronic schizophrenic, Tim attends
> classes at   City College of San Francisco. He is maintained
> on psychotropic drugs and has a primary therapist in a local
> community mental health clinic.   Tim reported that he had
> felt increasingly anxious, and that he had learned about
> group therapy through the school newspaper. He came to the
> student health clinic to arrange for an interview for
> admission to group. During this first meeting it was soon
> clear that   this student was not appropriate for this
> particular group membership.   He presented with a low
> attention span, tangential thinking, and loose associations,
> seemingly brought about by anxiety over beginnning the new
> semester. Because Tim´s ego functioning and ability to
> communicate were impaired he was not considered for this
> group due to his potential for regression and disruption.

> Referred by his instructor, Mark arrived for his first
> appointment under the influence of alcohol. Although not
> overly incoherent, his capacity for interaction in this
> session was impaired. The second interview revealed that
> although not intoxicated, the student´s ability to modulate
> his anger was ineffective to the extent that he was unable
> to provide details of family background without angry
> suspicion regarding the motives of the therapist.

> Jane was a recently divorced woman in her fifties with two
> dependent children. She was referred by a school nurse.
> Her presented concerns included her eligibility for public
> assistance while maintaining her status in school. She was
> also in need of legal aid concerning her divorce and medical
> referrals to assess diabetic symptoms.   As the interview
> proceeded, and the woman gained an understanding of the
> goals of the group, it became apparent to her and to the
> leaders that her needs could be better served through legal,
> medical and social work referrals rather than through group
> process at this time. This was thoroughly discussed during
> the second interview, to clarify the student´s aims, and she
> concluded that it was not group therapy that she required.

132

The preceding cases demonstrate some students who were not deemed appropriate for group. Tim, considered too dysfunctional to be included in group, was referred back to his primary therapist. Mark was deferred for group for the present time, and was referred, instead, to A.A. and to individual treatment in the community. While Jane made the decision not to join group at the time, the interview process was helpful to her in clarifying her needs and in directing her to the right resources.

Taking into account the expectable 20% attrition rate in most groups, we selected twelve students from our pool of applicants. Therefore, even if two or three members dropped out of the group, experience suggests that the number remaining is an optimal ratio for intimacy and individual and group interrelations.

The composition of this group of students seemed ideal both in terms of issues and in terms of personalities. These students shared concerns which involved school and relationships, and displayed personalities which appeared compatible. Overall, we found the members to be both curious and self-disclosing. They were willing to expose weaknesses before a peer group, and were tolerant of tension aroused by the hostile expression of others. They possessed a desire for mutuality of experience.

FACTORS THAT CONTRIBUTE TO A POSITIVE GROUP OUTCOME

The sharing of concerns and the concomitant identification with others'pain seems to lay the groundwork for trust and hope in group. For the college group, when concerns involve school related problems, identification in the form of camaraderie seems to be the first step toward group cohesion and for group work to begin. The growing recognition in group that problems and emotions are universal, and not unique to the individual, is enormously relieving. Acceptance by others, as well as the hope instilled by the discovery that "we're all in the same boat," is among the most healing benefits which group has to provide. This sharing of deepest concerns creates a group cohesiveness and bonding which allows the member to withstand strong expressions of anger and other emotions in an atmosphere which feels supportive and safe.

Another valuable part of the curative process of group (although not necessarily an end in itself), is the cathartic release engendered by the expression of emotion and experience.

Perhaps for most group members one of the most basic and valuable experiences is in interpersonal learning and communication. For the members at City College this experience

133

is invaluable given the variety of backgrounds from which the students come.

Group interaction develops socializing techniques and promotes insight and imitative behavior as well as the exchange of information and feedback. In the course of group sessions, students relate personal memories, stories and experiences which serve to foster collaborative exploration. It is in this context that the students' experience is, at least, two-fold, and that the true meaning of what it is to be a student on a community college campus becomes apparent. That is, when stories are recounted about academic situations, every member seems to relate immediately to some degree. There is a "sameness" of experience which engenders trust and group cohesiveness with little or no work to be done. However, when the stories are cultural, ethnic and family-bound, at first glance members are non-participating observers, but with little work, they begin relating at different levels to their own unique cultural and family experiences. What at first seemed isolating and different, fairly soon becomes a recognizable norm.

Individual differences can be a complex matter: not everyone needs the same things, or responds the same way in group. However, the very fact of individual differences can add to the potency of the group and become the agent of change for the members. For instance, as Yalom (1970) states, "... group members ... perceive the meaning of an event in exceedingly different ways... (regarding)... the importance of catharsis; many restricted individuals are benefitted by experiencing and expressing strong affect. Others, with contrasting problems of impulse control and great emotional lability may, on the contrary, profit from acquiring an intellectual structure and from reining in emotional expression. Some narcissistic characters need to learn to share and to give (altruism), while others, self-defeating in their retiring self-effacement, need to learn to ask for and demand their rights. Most likely, the manner in which an individual is helped in group therapy is the resultant of the interplay of several factors: his interpersonal needs, his strengths and weaknesses, his extra-group resources, and the composition and culture of his particular therapy group."

THE ADVANTAGES OF GROUP PARTICIPATION FOR STUDENTS ON A COMMUNITY COLLEGE CAMPUS

There are several advantages for students who attend group on campus. What seems most important to us is the student status and the campus community. That is, identification with fellow students provides a normative baseline from which to begin to share academic, sexual, home and family concerns in a safe and unthreatening environment. Also, there is a unique and readily accessible opportunity since group is held in a central location on campus: the student does not have to apply much effort or go very far to attend group sessions. Of particular importance to students is the no-fee provision of group services at school.

DISADVANTAGES OF PARTICIPATION FOR STUDENTS ON A COMMUNITY COLLEGE CAMPUS

The overriding disadvantage for students´ participating in group therapy on the campus is related to the physical setting of the community college and the issue of confidentiality and anonymity. While confidentiality can be established at once through the adherence by group members to group rules, anonymity cannot be so easily assured. In fact, unlike the person who is attending group therapy in a section of a town or city where the liklihood of seeing other members outside of group is minimal, students in college psychotherapy groups contend with constant encounters with other group members who attend classes with them or are around the campus at any given time. In this light, the issue of anonymity should be dealt with early in the group to allay resistance to disclosure by members.

Another critical disadvantage is that the group runs on the semester system, which entails many interruptions. All holidays are observed and the school closes at such times. Some holidays such as Winter Break are quite lengthy. These interruptions can be difficult for some students, evoking issues and feelings which must be dealt with on a continuing basis.

In addition, because group is part of the Student Health Service, which is closed evenings and weekends, therapists are not available during such times. Therefore, students are made aware of local community resources that provide services in emergencies and crises.

ADVANTAGES OF GROUP VS. INDIVIDUAL TREATMENT

At the most basic level, a greater number of students can receive therapy than if only individual treatment was offered. On a more personal level, for those students for whom individual therapy holds negative connotations, a group may be seen as more of a social microcosm in which they can work on mutual concerns. Oftentimes, a student´s interest in therapy is sparked by a psychology class at school, but the negative association with individual work may keep the student from pursuing the idea. Students who are unenlightened about therapy often discuss individual therapy in the context of having to be "crazy" to be in treatment. Whereas, many of these same students envision

135

group as a place to just go in order to learn to communicate or relate, and therefore, see group as a less threatening situation.

DISADVANTAGES OF GROUP THERAPY VS. INDIVIDUAL THERAPY

Although group therapy offers many benefits for students, there are some inherent limitations in group when compared to individual therapy. There is less intense focus and personal attention from the therapist in group, thus a reticent person may have his/her concerns overlooked. Also, there is less opportunity to work on individual ambivalence and resistance. Therefore, premature termination is not as easily forestalled.

CONCLUSION

Developing and establishing a psychotherapy group on the community college campus can be time-consuming and detailed work. But when all runs smoothly and successfully, group can be enormously satisfying, beneficial and rewarding for all concerned.

The group setting provides an opportunity for students to work on mutual concerns around issues of separation/individuation which aid in consolidating identity and self-esteem and functioning, both in academic and personal life.

Perhaps for the student of the community college the most important benefit that group can offer is a chance to work on issues that may be the crucial factors for remaining in school. This has broad social implications with regard to such issues as work and career eligibility and employment. Further, group may act as a catalyst and springboard for further growth and work where needed. This, coupled with the possible success in school and the development of social skills learned in group, assists the student to reenter the world in a more confident manner.

REFERENCES

Cohen, A.R. Situational Structure, Self Esteem and Threat-Oriented Reactions to Power. In D. Cartwright (Ed.) Studies in Social Power (Ann Arbor, Mich.: Research Center for Group Dynamics) 1959, p. 35-52.

Leopold, H. Selection of Patients for Group Psychotherapy. American Journal of Psychotherapy, 11 (1957) 634-637.

Mullen, H. & Rosenbaum, M. Group Psychotherapy. New York: Free Press of Glencove, 1962.

Saretsky,T. Active Techniques and Group Psychotherapy. New York: Jason Aronson, Inc., 1977.

Whitaker, D. & Lieberman H. Psychotherapy Through the Group Process. New York: Atherton Press, 1964.

Yalom, I.D. The Theory and Practice of Group Psychotherapy. New York: Basic Books, Inc., 1970.

THE EDITOR

Gerald Amada is Co-Director of the Mental Health Program, City College of San Francisco. He has served as a consultant to several task forces dealing with the emotionally disturbed and disruptive student for the Chancellor's Office of the California Community Colleges. Currently, Dr. Amada is also a member of the book review staff of American University Press, the American Journal of Psychotherapy and the San Francisco Chronicle.

Dr. Amada received his M.S.W. from Rutgers University and his Ph.D. in social and clinical psychology from the Wright Institute in Berkeley, California. He has authored three books, the last of which is entitled A Guide to Psychotherapy (Madison Books). In addition to his college-related activities, Dr. Amada has been a consultant to private industry.

In 1984, Dr. Amada received the Award of Excellence, category of administrator, post-secondary education, conferred by the National Association Vocational Educational Special Needs Personnel for Region 5, which comprises eighteen states.

Dr. Amada has a private psychotherapy practice in Mill Valley, California.

$20.00